the river

a memoir

by

Kevin Weadock

Copyright © 2019 by Kevin S. Weadock

All rights reserved. No parts of this publication may be reproduced, stored in a retrieval system, or transmitted in any form or by any means, electronic, mechanical, photocopying, recording, or otherwise, without the prior written permission of the copyright owner.

This book is sold subject to the condition that it shall not, by way of trade or otherwise, be lent, resold, hired out, or otherwise circulated without the publisher's prior consent in any form of binding or cover other than that in which it is published and without a similar condition including this condition being imposed on the subsequent purchaser. Under no circumstances may any part of this book be photocopied for resale.

The stories in this memoir reflect the author's recollection of events. Some names and identifying details have been changed to protect the privacy of those depicted. Dialogue has been re-created from memory.

ISBN: 9781724083623

"Hope" is the thing with feathers –
That perches in the soul –
And sings the tune without the words –
And never stops – at all –

And sweetest – in the Gale – is heard –
And sore must be the storm –
That could abash the little Bird
That kept so many warm –

I've heard it in the chillest land –
And on the strangest Sea –
Yet – never – in Extremity,
It asked a crumb – of me.

- Emily Dickinson

1

My father worked in skyscrapers. When work was over, he belted down a few shots of whiskey and took the A train home to our bungalow on 44th Street in Rockaway Beach. He wore the same clothes every day: black work boots dusted with white powder, blue jeans held up by a black belt, and a white T-shirt covered by a light gray jacket. He smoked a Camel cigarette as he walked home from the subway station and spat out little pieces of tobacco along the way.

The first thing my father did when he got home was fling his jacket on the couch. He then assumed his position on a beaten-up recliner in front of our television. My father had plenty of silly names for us. My six-year-old brother Mickey was the "Snipper Snacker," my four-year-old brother Dennis was the "Dinny Doon," and I was the "Kinder Connor." My father added a small black dog named Finnegan to our family as well. Irish names were important to my father, who was born in Ireland on St. Patrick's Day.

"Who wants to get their poor old father a beer?" he asked us, leaning back in his chair.

While one of us ran to get a can of Schaefer out of the refrigerator, two of us loosened the laces of his boots and wrestled them off his feet. There was even more fun in smelling his socks.

"That's worse than yesterday!" announced my seven-year-old brother, Paddy.

"Now you smell them, Kevin," Mickey insisted.

"Arghh!"

"I want to smell them, too," chimed Dennis.

"Arghh!"

Amidst all this fun and commotion, one or two of us might sneak a sip of beer—with the hope of getting a foam mustache.

From the kitchen, my mother warned, "Don't let them touch those socks, Pat!"

"Don't worry honey, they're just having a little fun. Now, who wants to get their poor old father another beer?"

And so it went.

2

Paddy's job was to take the Indian Head nickel that my father handed him each night and go to the deli near the subway station to buy a newspaper called *The Journal*. I viewed the job as a big responsibility, one that only Paddy could have. Because I was just five years old, Paddy was almost like a man to me. His hair was dark like my father's, and he stood at least six inches taller than me.

I sometimes pretended that I was a man, and imitated my father's return from work. I walked down to the subway station and waited for passengers to step off the train. Equipped with a serious face, acting like I just got back from my job, I mixed into the pack of people and then headed home. I stuck my chest out a little and spread my arms. Everyone was surely looking through their windows, marveling at my manliness.

Many of the bungalows on our street had dune roses in front of their porches. These roses smelled like regular roses mixed with cinnamon. We had tiger lilies and May bells in front of *our* porch. I was drawn to the beauty of the May bells. I looked at the tiny white flowers as closely as I could, smelled them, and held them up to the sun. I was amazed that nature had created flowers to imitate manmade bells.

Jamaica Bay was a quarter-mile away on one end of our street, and Rockaway Beach was a half-mile away in the opposite direction. The sound of airplanes flying to and from nearby Kennedy Airport was nonstop. From our bungalow's porch I watched the planes float and wobble in the sky as they approached the airport. I wondered how such huge things could float in the air.

The rain gutter above our porch had a sparrow's nest in it. A few of the baby sparrows once fell out of the nest and onto the ground. My mother picked them up with her bare hands and brought them to our kitchen table. She laid them on a small rag and taught me how to feed them with an eye dropper filled with milk and tiny bits of bread.

Our porch was also the place where my father held me in his arms on one Christmas Eve. He pointed up to the moon with his free hand and told me that Rudolph and all the other reindeer were going to pull Santa Claus and his sleigh full of toys through the sky at midnight. I wondered how big Santa's sleigh would be compared to the planes that were flying by.

I frequently strayed from our porch to walk around the neighborhood. I wandered into various stores and alleys many blocks away. I once spent an afternoon watching a fire that started in a field on Edgemere Avenue and spread to the 44th Street subway station. The fire was as high as the tracks on the elevated subway train. Fire engines came from all directions with their sirens blasting. I was in a trance ... not thinking about the fire so much—but more amazed at the heights of the arcs of water being hosed into it. I walked as close as I could to the fire, only to be gobbled up by a crowd of grown-ups. I stayed at the scene until the fire trucks drove away.

When I didn't know where I was, I asked grown-ups to help me. Their help once resulted in me getting a ride in the back of a police car. I kicked and screamed and cried all the way home. The policeman let me out of his car and walked me over to a bunch of ladies who were standing outside our bungalow.

One of the ladies bent down and put her hand on my shoulder. "Your mom was in a car accident today, Kevin."

"She got hit by a car?" I asked.

"No, no, no … she was driving your father's car, and because she didn't want to run over a little puppy that was trying to cross the street, she crashed into one of the concrete columns that hold up the train tracks."

"Well, where's my mom now?"

"She's at Peninsula Hospital now, and the doctors are giving her medicine to help her feel better."

"Is she gonna die?"

"No, honey. She'll be home in a few more days, OK?"

Standing on our porch a few days later, I watched my father help my mother out of the back seat of a taxi. They fumbled with her crutches as the taxi drove away. My mother tried to keep her long brown hair out of her face as she struggled to walk with the crutches. When she got inside, she plopped down on our couch, exhausted. We gathered around her and bombarded her with questions.

"Is your leg broken or something, Mom?" asked Paddy.

"Yes, but it's going to get better, honey."

"Are the stitches holding your head together, Mom?" I asked.

"No, honey. It's just the skin that got hurt."

"Does it hurt?" asked Katie.

"I'm fine, Katie."

"Where's the puppy, Mom?" I asked. "Did it live?"

We were fascinated by the brace on her neck, the cast on her leg, and the big cut on her forehead. We took turns touching the cast, tapping it gently and getting a sense of its unusual texture. The big cut went through the center of her forehead—from her hairline to one of her eyebrows. It had lots of little black stitches in it. I worried that the stitches were the only thing holding her head together, and that if they failed, her head might crack open again.

My eight-year-old sister Katie now had to help my mother with all the cooking and cleaning. Katie had long brunette hair, and she was even taller than Paddy. She became just like another mom to me and my brothers. She taught us how to make sandwiches from white bread and sugar. Sometimes, we added butter and cinnamon. If we wanted to toast our bread, we put it on a fork and held it near the flame on the stove.

3

Our new home on the corner of Rockaway Beach Boulevard and 88th Street was one of three apartments above a butcher shop. The door to the apartments was just a foot to the left of the door to the butcher shop and led to a steep flight of stairs that ended at a landing on the second floor. The landing was poorly lit during the day, with only a small amount of light coming through a skylight in the building's roof. Getting to our apartment required walking past the other apartments and toward the back of the landing. The door to our apartment opened into our living room. The kitchen was on the left, and my parents' bedroom was behind that. All of us kids shared a big bedroom on the front side of our building, where the ocean air came in. We had two windows in our room that allowed us to see Rockaway Beach Boulevard below, a supermarket across the street, and Rockaway Beach off in the distance. My sister Donna was born a few months after we moved in.

The butcher shop had sawdust on the floor. Every time I went inside, I curiously eyed the huge chunks of meat and bone. The hairy-armed butcher let me stand around and watch him chop the meat with his butcher's knife. I was particularly interested in the cartilage that capped off some of the bones. The faint blue hue under the shiny white surface didn't seem to belong.

Along with big black flies, the smell of rotting meat in the garbage cans snuck into the back of our apartment. Countering this smell was the clean air coming off the ocean and into our front bedroom window.

Neighbors and friends of neighbors came into and out of our apartment whenever they wanted to. They were young and loud and smoked lots of cigarettes. My mother liked to drink Rheingold beer with them. Sometimes she forgot about us and left us alone in our apartment. One day, I was completely alone, sitting on my bed in the front bedroom. When I went to leave the room, a teenage girl and her boyfriend blocked the door. I had no idea who they were or why they were in our apartment. The girl stood behind the boyfriend, who was standing in front of me. She was laughing, and had her arms wrapped around his shoulders. Her skinny boyfriend wore a white T-shirt and blue jeans. He said the only way I could leave the room was to do what he told me to do. He then pulled his dick out of his pants.

On another day, I was alone on the second-floor landing and noticed an old woman gazing down through the skylight. She had long gray hair and was missing some teeth. She was trying to talk to me through the skylight's glass, but I couldn't hear her. She laughed as she spoke, and wagged her finger at me. Seemingly frustrated with me, she stood up so that her feet straddled the skylight. She was wearing a dirty white robe that looked like a bedsheet. She then pulled the robe up to her hips. I saw her underwear, which was wet near her crotch—like she had peed on herself. Frightened, I ran down the stairs to the street and frantically searched for my mother. After a while, I just stood in front of the butcher shop and waited for her to come home.

THE RIVER

"There's a witch on the roof, Mom!" I screamed.

"What? What do you mean, Kevin?"

I told my mother what I had seen in the skylight.

"Oh, Kevy, there's no such thing as witches. That must have been the crazy lady on the roof. She lives around here. She wouldn't hurt you, honey."

4

The more my parents drank, the more likely they would fight. When they did, my siblings and I hid in the front bedroom. While Katie and Paddy peeked out the door to watch, I usually hid under the blankets on our bed. I had seen enough to know that this was the safest place for me.

My father spit into my mother's face. He also liked to rip the phone cord out of the wall so she couldn't call the police. He had his usual barrage of slurs as well.

"You're a fucking cunt!"

"You dirty whore!"

"You fucking cocksucker!"

My mother threw pots and dishes at him. She hit him on his shoulders or back or wherever she could land a punch. She had names for him, too.

"You fucking bastard!"

"Motherfucker!"

"You're a son of a bitch!"

One of their fights involved my baby sister Donna.

"She's not mine, and you know it," my father accused. "There are no blonds in my family!"

"She sure as hell is!" my mother yelled as she pushed Donna into his arms.

My father plopped Donna on the bed and walked away.

"Take her back to her blond-haired father, you filthy fucking whore!"

My mother picked Donna up and handed her back to my father.

"Well, here you go, *Daddy*, you lying son of a bitch!"

One night, Paddy pulled me and my other siblings into the front bedroom.

"Guess what?" he asked us.

"What? What?" we all demanded.

"Dad made me watch Mom and some man kiss and hug each other. They were laying on the ground by the bridge."

That night, the fighting was so intense that my heart pounded under my pajama shirt. It only happened when they fought. I called it my "heart pounding problem." My parents were yelling and punching in the living room … and then in their bedroom. I heard a window or mirror break, and then their bedroom door burst open. The fight moved onto the landing outside our apartment door.

I heard a scream—followed by a long moment of silence. I'd experienced something similar in a prior fight of theirs. My mother had fought like a crazy street cat—until my father punched her in the stomach. Then there was only the sound of my father's footsteps fading away.

When I heard my mother's voice again, I ran to our front door and opened it. She was kneeling, with her face less than a foot from mine. The big cut from the car accident had reopened. Blood streamed down her face and out of her mouth.

"What happened, Mom?" I screamed.

In a weak garbled voice, she murmured, "Your father pushed me down the stairs, honey."

5

If it weren't for the headlights from cars, there wouldn't have been any light, anywhere. The rushing storm water was as high as my knees. My mother grabbed my wrist and pulled up so I could jump onto the curb. She held Donna with her other arm. Nearby cars and people were also trying to move through the water, and the wind and rain roared all around us. Katie was struggling to carry a large bag of bananas. My mother eventually got all six of us to the 90th Street subway station, and then on to an A train which took us to Penn Station, where we spent the night.

The train ride to Minnesota was a blur of looking out the windows and trying to sleep on the seats or on the floor between them.

"When are we going to be there?" we constantly asked my mother.

We arrived at our layover in Chicago in the middle of the night. I had never heard of Chicago before. I only knew it was far from Rockaway Beach. The train station was eerily quiet and almost empty. A large television placed high on the wall was in sign-off mode, displaying just a bunch of black circles on a white background. I sat on a wooden bench and ate a banana while my mother talked to a skinny black lady sitting next to us.

On the train from Chicago to Minnesota, we leaned our heads against the windows, ate bananas, and watched

THE RIVER

the countryside roll by—cows and fields and barns followed by cows and fields and barns followed by cows and fields and barns.

My maternal grandparents, Alma and Vernon Burns, met us as we got off the train in Minneapolis. They were tall and skinny, and their clothes draped off them. To get us all into their big old car, my mother had us lie down on the floor or find a place to sit. I chose to lie down on the back deck by the rear windshield. As we drove away, the sunlight barged through the glass and into my eyes. I played with a bobble-head German shepherd toy that had previously occupied the spot.

"Where are we going *now*, Mom?" Paddy demanded.

"We're going to visit Aunt Esther," she answered.

"Who's that?" I asked.

"She's *my* aunt, and she has her own farm, with cows and chickens."

"How far is it from here?" I asked.

"It's about one hundred miles away," my grandfather explained.

"How far is *that?*" I yelled.

After the storm and two train rides we just had, "one hundred" seemed like the longest distance anyone could ever travel. My grandfather tried to explain how far it was by showing me the odometer—but I still couldn't make sense of it. Paddy spent a good part of the ride trying to explain to me how big one hundred was as compared to ten and twenty-five and fifty. I learned that fourteen thousand was probably the largest number in the world, and the Sun was fourteen thousand miles away.

My great-Aunt Esther stood on the porch of her home as we pulled up in my grandfather's car. She was slightly hunched over and wore heavy clothes and an apron. She didn't say much to us—just a bunch of short sentences under her breath as she shuffled around the kitchen, opening cabinets and looking for food to put on the table.

We were too excited to sit inside the house with old people—and darted outside instead. I had never seen or smelled anything like a farm. Even in the cold air, the stench of cow manure threatened to overwhelm me. Uncle Mike, my mother's younger brother, was excited by our visit and quickly gave us a tour. We did our best to follow the tall, skinny blond man from one end of the farm to the other. He brought us into the barn, which was only about fifty yards from the house. We saw cows lined up in two rows—each row separated by a concrete walkway. The cows had their asses facing us, and as we moved down the walkway, I was afraid one of the cows might kick me. At the end of the walkway was a huge cage with bars like a jail cell. Inside the cage was a gigantic bull, and I was terrified of the power it had. I then noticed a mouse walking along the edges of the bull's cage. I was equally afraid of the mouse.

Uncle Mike carried a big metal pail of warm milk from the barn right into the kitchen. He poured some into a cup and asked me if I wanted to taste "real milk."

I hated it.

There was also a young blonde girl, some sort of cousin to me, who walked around the farm. She showed me around one of the other old buildings next to the main barn.

"I'm nine years old," she proudly told me.

The next thing I heard was, "I have to pee."

She grabbed a rusty coffee can from the side of the building, pulled down her pants, and peed into the can.

6

We were a hot potato. After a few days at the farm, we went to live at my Aunt Linda's apartment for a week or so, then on to a vacant bungalow owned by someone my grandmother knew. The bungalow was in a town called Mound, and it sat just up a hill from a lake that had many houses lining its shore.

An outhouse that looked like a wooden phone booth stood just ten yards away from the bungalow. Its roof was slanted, and the siding was made of vertical planks of waterlogged wood. It wasn't long before I had to use it. When I opened the door, I saw a bench with two holes in it. I pulled my pants down, sat on top of one of the holes, and tried not to breathe in the disgusting gases rising from below.

The owner renovated the bungalow while we lived in it. About a dozen wooden beams, each nearly a foot thick, were placed under the bungalow so a basement could be formed by excavating the dirt beneath it. A huge yellow bulldozer was parked outside, and we played on the machine when the workers went home. The smells of newly exposed dirt and clay were strong in and around the bungalow. One day, the man driving the bulldozer told my mother we weren't supposed to be living in the bungalow while it was being elevated. She argued with him until he left.

When the weather warmed up, I started to play by the lake down the hill from the bungalow. I fell in love with a small dock that was about three feet wide and twenty feet long. The dock quickly became the best place in my life. I loved to lie down at the end and feel the sun on my back as I watched the fish swim underneath. The water was clear and only about three feet deep.

My Uncle Mike noticed I liked to play on the dock. He gave me a few feet of fishing line and a small hook and showed me how to fish. I placed a small piece of bread on the hook and hung my arm over the dock, dragging the bait toward any visible prey. When I felt a little tug on the line, my heart skipped a beat ... I'd soon have a fish. I learned to trim small tree branches and use them to toss longer lines out into deeper water. I also used a red-and-white bobber to see if a fish was biting.

Mickey soon noticed the action on the dock and joined in with his own hook and line. Mickey and I seemed to be together most times. The fact that we were brothers wasn't initially obvious. He was stocky and had black hair and brown eyes. I was skinny with light brown hair and green eyes. Other than that, we were identical twins. We even jumped off the dock and into the lake at the same time!

Minnesota had lots of flowers with blazing orange and purple colors. It had plenty of ponds as well—all with lily pads and branches, frogs and turtles sitting and diving, fish darting beneath the lilies, and a range of smells that were new to us. We liked to walk along the lakeshore, and occasionally into the woods, looking for who knows what.

One night, Mickey and I wound up in an area where there were large homes. They had long curvy driveways and sat high above the lake. We walked right up close to one home that had fancy bushes and flowers surrounding

THE RIVER

it. We peeked through a huge window and saw people sitting and talking on a big couch. It seemed like we were watching a movie about rich people and fireplaces and fancy stuff.

Sometime after that night, Mickey told me he had looked into a window of a lakefront bungalow near the dock where we played.

"There's nobody in it!" he reported.

"So?" I challenged.

"Let's go in it and get fishing stuff!"

Mickey was seven years old, and I was six. Minutes after getting into the bungalow, Mickey found a hammer and used it to start smashing everything around him.

I joined in.

We broke lamps and mirrors and windows. I climbed on a chair that was on one side of a dining room cabinet loaded with fancy cups and dishes. Mickey climbed on a chair placed near the other side. We pushed the cabinet over, breaking the glass and most of the china that spilled onto the floor. We emptied out the drawer of silverware and knocked more furniture over. We then went outside and broke more windows. We finished by emptying a toolbox into the lake and sinking a small rowboat that was attached to their dock.

7

The Gibsons owned a large three-story house on Lake Minnetonka. Beautiful gardens of begonias and fragrant roses lined the sprawling lakefront property. My grandmother was a maid for the Gibsons, and my grandfather worked part-time as a gardener for them. The Gibson's house had a huge kitchen—and a couple of other people cooked and cleaned in there.

The Gibsons let my family stay over a few times. We stayed for a couple of days each time, and they even let my Uncle Mike take us fishing on their rowboat. He woke us up before dawn to collect worms. While he held a flashlight behind us, we used kitchen spoons to dig in the dirt by the flower garden. We threw the worms into a rusty coffee can and got onto the boat as the sun rose. As we motored out into the deepest portions of the lake, I realized that, except for my parents, my entire family was on the little boat. We were all afraid to move or do anything else that might tip us over.

The Gibsons allowed us to wander freely about their property and beautiful house. After waking from a nap I took in a bedroom on the top floor of the home, I looked through a window near the side of the bed. Soft classical music coming from one of the other rooms seemed to match the scene outside. A warm breeze fluttered through the white lace curtains, and I was in a trance

THE RIVER

again—watching puffy clouds drift slowly in the sky above the lake. A dense wall of tall pine trees lined the distant shore. My mother and her sisters were with my siblings, gathered around a picnic table beneath the window. I could hear them talking and laughing. I closed my eyes and made a wish that the Gibsons would let us live there.

8

Winter was too cold for us to continue living in the bungalow by the lake. We had to move in with my Aunt Donna, my mother's oldest sibling, in downtown Minneapolis. She had dark brown hair and wore ruby-red lipstick and lived in a one-bedroom apartment with a narrow galley kitchen. It was on the second floor of a building on a bustling street—with a bus stop right at the base of the stairs. Petula Clark's "Downtown" was a hit on the radio, and it captured exactly what was going on in our lives—now that we lived near all the excitement *downtown*.

One day, Aunt Donna left all of us kids alone in her apartment while she went to get my mother from a hospital somewhere. We stayed in the living room, watching television and eating sandwiches we made from white bread and sugar. Late that night, my mother and Aunt Donna came home from the hospital with my baby brother Timothy. He was so little—I was afraid to touch him. There were seven of us now, and while my mother lay on the couch, she held him in a blue wool blanket. Aunt Donna made trays of little milk bottles in the kitchen.

Christmas came about a month after Timmy was born. Our Christmas tree smelled great and had plenty of lights and tinsel and an angel perched at the top. On Christmas Eve, we laid on the floor near the tree and wondered if Santa Claus could put presents under the tree without waking us up. The glistening tinsel and sugary sweet colors of the Christmas lights promised magic and excitement just ahead. We stayed awake for as long as we could, peeking at the tree and out of the windows to see if Santa was nearby. We woke up early on Christmas morning—only to see there were no gifts under the tree. My mother cried as she told us there was no such thing as Santa Claus.

Later that day, I sensed a commotion in Aunt Donna's kitchen. My mother was there with her parents and siblings, laughing about a Christmas gift Aunt Donna had given her—a Matchbox car with a folded-up dollar bill taped to the top of it.

9

The drive back to Rockaway Beach took two days. Except for Timmy, all of us kids sat in the back seat. Timmy slept in a cardboard box that was placed on the front seat, next to my mother. Katie helped my mom change his diapers. My grandfather drove, and he and my mother drank beer the whole way back.

Along the way, we stopped at a Sinclair gas station to get toy dinosaurs—promotional items given to customers who filled up their tanks. Each of us got a "Dino the Dinosaur" brontosaurus, which was green and plastic and about four inches tall. We all agreed that Dino was our Christmas present.

We arrived at our 96th Street apartment on an overcast New Year's Eve. My siblings and I ran up the porch steps and into the apartment. On the left was a small living room that had a couch, a black-and-white television sitting on a small table, and a large black chest that stored my father's tools—the usual assortment of hammers, levels, and wood planers. Wood shavings littered the inside of the trunk and the floor next to it. The kitchen and bathroom were tucked behind this small room. The stairs to the right of the entrance led up to the bedrooms on the second floor. Each of the rooms had an old wooden dresser and a large mattress on the floor. Steam radiators hissed as I tugged the string that turned the ceiling mounted light bulb on.

THE RIVER

When we were done with our quick look at the apartment, we walked side by side down 96th Street, toward the ocean. Nobody else was on the street. The boardwalk was only half a block away, and the ocean was right behind that. The cold ocean air invigorated me, and I heard the waves crashing ahead of us. I was back at my *real* home—Rockaway Beach.

As we walked, Paddy started talking about how great the Beatles were. We talked about which Beatle had the longest hair and tried to remember their names. All *I* knew was Ringo played the drums.

While we were at the beach, my grandfather left. He didn't even say goodbye to us. My father came home later that night. My mother met him at the door with open arms. They hugged and cried right in front of us.

10

It took a while for us to get used to the cold and empty apartment. We kept busy by playing with my father's tools. My favorite tool was a ruler that folded in all sorts of ways. I stretched it out to its fullest extent and measured the size of the rooms and refrigerator. I also measured the heights of my brothers as they lay on the floor. For additional entertainment, we melted crayons on the radiators in our rooms. We pressed the crayons onto the top of the hot iron and let gravity do the rest. The crayons smelled great as they dripped down the sides of the radiators. We used different colors to make whatever designs we wanted. It was like our own little art class up there, with the radiators as our canvases.

We also watched the first *Batman* television show ever made. When the opening music started, we jumped up and down in our pajamas, doing all the "POW" and "ZAP" punches together. The volume of the television was so high we could barely hear each other scream. We were flushed with adrenalin, and I enjoyed seeing my brothers' faces light up with maniacal joy as we jumped off the back of the couch. I was so inspired by Batman and Robin I started to dress up at night as my own superhero: *Whiteman!* I had white underwear, a white T-shirt tucked into my underwear, white socks, and a white towel for a cape. I pretended to fly by jumping off the couch, and I walked around the apartment with my chest puffed out. Even my brothers thought I had gone too far.

An elderly couple, who were somehow aware of our recent arrival to 96th Street, offered to let all of us kids watch *The Wizard of Oz* on their *color* television. We huddled in front of the screen and waited for the movie to start. I was immediately entranced. When Dorothy opened her front door after landing in Oz, the scene switched from black-and-white to color. Dorothy's experience was just like ours—her life and house could suddenly be blown into the air. The intensity of the movie rattled me. If Toto wasn't in the movie, I would have run back home.

11

My father soon bought us bicycles. Dennis and I shared a green two-wheeler with training wheels. Katie, Paddy, and Mickey shared a larger red bike. The training wheels on our green bike came off the first day I rode it. I didn't want training wheels, so Paddy told me to sit on the bike and lean against the fence across our street. He held me up, and as I started pedaling, he let go of me. I fell over a few times, but was soon riding it everywhere. I rarely came home. I rode from Jamaica Bay to the ocean and for many blocks up and down Rockaway Beach.

One winter day, I was riding my bike near the 98th Street subway station. I must not have been paying attention to oncoming traffic or the presence of ice on the road. When I realized a car was coming from my left, I jammed on my brake, causing the bike to slip on the ice and slide right into the car. My head and shoulder got lodged beneath the car, near the front side of the rear right wheel.

Fortunately, the driver had applied his own brakes just in time. From my view under the car, I saw his feet rush around the front of his car toward me.

"Oh my God! Are you OK?" he screamed.

"Yeah, I'm OK," I announced from under the car.

As he pulled me out, he was still frantic—yelling "Oh my God!"

THE RIVER

He reached into his wallet and gave me three dollars. He then jumped back into his car and drove away.

We eventually met other kids on 96th Street. The first kid I met was Drew, who lived in the house directly across the street from our apartment. Drew had red hair and was almost a teenager. He liked to squeeze my hands as hard as he could until I cried.

Bonnie Walker lived on 96th Street too. Bonnie was my age and had dark eyes and long brunette hair tied in a ponytail. We occasionally found ourselves standing next to one another on the street, and we even started to talk. Paddy noticed this happening and said we should get married. He ran into our apartment and brought out a comic book. He told Bonnie and me to hold hands while he pretended to read wedding vows. Bonnie and I both felt awkward about the whole scene, but a small crowd of kids gathered around us to enjoy it. A few days later, Bonnie and I went walking near some large forsythia bushes lining the side of the boardwalk. We wanted to kiss each other "in private," so we ducked between the bushes and the boardwalk and crouched down together. We kissed for a second—and then I gave Bonnie a hard smack in the face with my hand. I had an inexplicable urge to do it. Bonnie ran away, never to play with me again.

I tried playing with other kids on our street, but soon learned their mothers didn't want them near me. This confused me because one of those mothers had found me on the street late one night and brought me into her apartment to sleep on her couch. Her kids didn't talk to me when I went to the bus stop. One day, my siblings and I were the last kids to get on the school bus. Since there were no seats left, we had to stand in the aisle. When the bus started moving, the other kids started singing a stinging melody:

> *"Weadocks, your cooties stink!"*
> *"Weadocks, your cooties stink!"*
> *"Weadocks, your cooties stink!"*

We were stunned with embarrassment. It seemed like they had rehearsed it before we got on the bus. I thought the only kids who knew my name lived on 96th street—but I was wrong. After that day, we frequently played hooky on the beach. We hid under the boardwalk until school was over. I missed so many days of second grade that I had no idea what was going on when I did attend.

The school bus ride back home stopped across the street from Playland. Instead of going directly home, I lost myself inside the noise and chaos of the amusement park. On other days, I walked a few blocks past our apartment to go to the 100th precinct. I'd just meander in and say hello to the policemen behind the high desk. I liked them because they broke up fights between my parents.

12

The bay side of Rockaway Beach was less than a mile from the ocean. The numbered streets ran perpendicular to Rockaway Beach Boulevard. Rockaway Playland, an amusement park, was just two blocks away. I earned my way on the rides by running errands for the ride operators. They gave me their loose change to fetch them a soda, a slice of pizza, or a newspaper.

Playland housed the usual collection of attractions—a fun house, Tilt-A-Whirl, Ferris wheel, and various games of chance. But nothing came close to the excitement and fear elicited by the Atom Smasher—an old wooden roller coaster that roared all day and into the night. The Atom Smasher was separated from the 98th Street sidewalk by ten feet of space and a chain-link fence. From the sidewalk, I could easily see and hear the thunderous roller coaster's main drop, the cars' comings and goings, and the rider's screams. To me, the Atom Smasher was as significant as the ocean and the moon. Its first ascent went straight up to a rounded turn that gave a full view of the ocean. The coaster then dropped sharply to street level and followed with a long slow march up to its peak. The Atom Smasher then roared as it stormed downward. This part of the ride made me close my eyes and grip the crossbar. I feared the Atom Smasher might come off the tracks or throw me to the street below. The coaster then tore through a series of wild turns and drops before it was done with me. The sound of the brakes let me know I would live another day.

Dennis and I shared a bed in the back bedroom, which was close to 97th Street. In the summer months, we left our windows open to let in the cool ocean air and smells of cotton candy and funnel cake. We fell asleep listening to the screams of people riding the roaring Atom Smasher.

The bay itself was another playground of sorts for me. The Cross Bay Bridge connecting Rockaway Beach to the rest of New York City was just a few blocks from our apartment. I liked to spend time on the bridge with the older men who fished there. If I went to the bait shop at the base of the bridge to fetch anchors, bait, cigarettes, and other stuff for them, they gave me money to buy soda.

I once noticed thick schools of mackerel swimming in water at the base of the bridge near the bait shop. Some bigger kids and I waded into the chest-high water to try to catch them with our hands. The excitement of catching mackerel with just our hands drove us all into a frenzy. The fish were so close to me—I could easily see the stripes on their backs as they swam just a foot below the surface of the water. While the bigger kids had already caught a few, I had merely felt one slip through my hands. I wanted to catch one *by myself*, away from the bossy bigger kids. I spied another spot that had some fish swimming around—it was near a concrete dock just fifty yards away. I naively stepped off the dock and backed down over rocks that were covered with seaweed, causing me to slip into the bay. The current immediately pulled me away from the rocks.

In a wild panic, I started splashing my arms in a swimming motion—but quickly sank beneath the surface. In all my passes under the dock on the lake in Minnesota, I had learned to move my arms underwater to propel myself forward. This instinct didn't kick in when my head was above water, but it miraculously *did* kick in when I went under. Within seconds, one of my hands caught the edge of a rock, allowing me to resist the pull of the current. I quickly used my other hand to grab another rock edge to pull myself up and get my head out of the water. I eventually climbed back onto the concrete dock.

The ocean wasn't as forgiving as the bay. One afternoon, I was standing in shallow water formed by a sandbar, which sometimes occurred during low tide and allowed me to walk way out into the ocean. I suddenly became aware of two lifeguards running directly toward me—only to alter their run at the last second and head into the deeper area. Within minutes, they carried a teenage girl out of the ocean and onto the beach, where they dumped her on someone's blanket. I ran back to the beach and saw she was unconscious and wearing a white polka-dot bikini. A small crowd of people gathered around to watch the lifeguards try to save her with mouth-to-mouth resuscitation.

"Where's her family?!" the lifeguards yelled.

"*Where* is her family?!"

Nobody knew.

Her body just stayed limp—there was no sign of life that *I* could see. Each lifeguard then picked up two corners of the blanket so it acted like a hammock for the girl. They rushed her to an ambulance waiting on the boardwalk. The people who had gathered to watch the rescue attempt just walked away.

13

My father didn't trust my mother with money. He thought she would spend it on beer instead of feeding us. So, before he went to work each day, he gave Katie two dollars to buy a quart of milk and a box of Sweet Sixteen donuts from the deli down the street. We each got two donuts and a small paper cup of milk for breakfast. We ate cereal for many meals during the day. For milk, we combined rust-colored water from the faucet with powdered milk.

After work, my father went straight to one or more Irish bars in the neighborhood—and stayed there until he was drunk. By the time he came home, my mother might also be drunk or in the process of getting drunk. If my mother was sober, she cooked things like chili or chicken fricassee for dinner and made fudge or apple crisp for dessert. If dinner wasn't made by the time my father got home, he gave Katie three dollars to go to the pizzeria around the corner to buy a pizza pie and a large bottle of soda.

Nonetheless, I was frequently hungry and occasionally looked for food in the garbage cans at Playland or on the beach. The cans in Playland offered left-over cotton candy and pizza crusts. The cans on the beach were made from metal and had repeating diagonal cutouts so the ocean couldn't drag them away. This pattern made it easy for me to see what was in the cans: remnants of sandwiches, open boxes of Cracker Jacks, and parts of hot dogs—all hidden to some degree by bottles and cans and wrinkled up paper bags. Some rich person even threw out a ham and cheese sandwich with spicy mustard. They had taken just a few bites.

14

The hall on the landing at the top of the stairs of our 96th Street apartment had two bedrooms on one side and my parents' bedroom on the other, just above the stairwell. I never went into their room.

While walking up the stairs one afternoon, I squinted to avoid getting hit in the eyes by the sunlight coming in from the back-facing window at the top of the landing. When I got to the second floor, I turned the corner and walked toward the front of the house. As I did, I saw a gray suit jacket and pants hanging on the doorknob to my parents' bedroom. The pants had a black belt attached, and the pockets to the suit were ruffled slightly open. I had occasionally stolen change from my father's pants and was tempted to dig into these pockets as well—but I sensed the pants were not my father's. I quietly walked back down the stairs.

My parents fought that night, and my father was so upset he stormed out of the apartment. While he was out, Katie, who was ten years old, baked him a cake in a square pan—a chocolate Betty Crocker cake with chocolate frosting. We were all excited about giving it to my father when he came home. We hoped it would make him happy. He eventually did come back home—angry and drunk. When Katie presented the cake to him, the rest of us were sitting on the couch in the front room, watching television.

THE RIVER

My father took the cake from her and flung it hard against the wall, just above the television. Katie stood on a spot halfway up the stairs, leaning her arms on the bannister. She was trembling, looking down at my father as he yelled at my mother about some man with an Irish last name. I never told my father I saw the suit hanging on the door.

15

My father was the youngest of nine siblings born into a prominent family from Arklow, a seaside town just fifty miles south of Dublin. All but one of his older siblings eventually left Ireland to settle in New York City, where they became successful in real estate and other endeavors. His older sister was our Aunt Sis. She owned a three-story house on 95th Street. The house had a bar called Connolly's located on the ground floor. She also owned a second three-story house next door. During the summer months, she rented out rooms in the second house.

Behind these two homes were wooden shower stalls beachgoers used to wash sand off their bodies. One day, I heard fire engines near our apartment on 96th Street, and I ran to where they were. Firemen were fighting a blaze in the backyard of a house across the street from us, just behind my Aunt's house. A shed located just behind the showers was burning. I watched the fire trucks for a while ... and the firemen and their hoses ... and the water arc into the air. Some of the cold water streamed back toward the curb, under my bare feet, and into the sewer drain. I heard people in the crowd saying that my brother Mickey started the fire. I was certain he was being blamed for something he didn't do.

Mickey later admitted to me that he did set the fire between the shed and shower. He said that while he was

THE RIVER

taking a shower to get sand off his body, a naked man entered the stall and forced him to get naked too. He told me how mean the man was to him in the shower.

16

I stopped my bike in front of the pizzeria that was across the street from Playland. I watched the truck carry our furniture and stuff towards our next apartment. The truck had slatted wood railings that enabled me to see our pee-stained mattresses, junky dressers and chairs, and flimsy cardboard boxes holding our clothes and everything else. I was afraid the kids who teased us on the bus might see it too. Traffic was heavy, and the truck couldn't move fast enough for me. I wanted it gone. I followed it all the way to 115th Street.

Our new apartment was less than fifty yards from the boardwalk. It was on the second floor of a home that shared a courtyard with four other families. My family was suddenly living in a fishbowl, giving the whole neighborhood a front-row seat to the craziness that consumed us. The neighbors saw and heard everything. They even knew my mother was sent to the hospital one time for drinking too much and acting crazy.

One afternoon, I was walking in the courtyard after coming home from the beach. As I approached the entrance to our apartment, Katie came running down the stairs. She was holding one of her hands, which was bleeding badly, and she ran past me—yelling for help. She'd been feeding Donna and Timmy in their high chairs, and Mickey had been whirling around the kitchen with a knife in his hand.

THE RIVER

Fearing Mickey was too close to the kids, she tried to get the knife away from him. She grabbed the blade edge just as Mickey was pulling it away, and the knife cut through her palm.

It was moments like this that made it hard for me to figure out whether it was better to be at home, on the beach, or on the street somewhere in the neighborhood. I frequently wound up on the corner of 115th Street and Rockaway Beach Boulevard, which was just a hundred yards from our apartment. That's where I got hit by a red Corvette as I was crossing the street. Although the car was moving at barely five miles per hour, the low front bumper struck me behind my knees, causing them to slam down hard on the pavement. I stood up, looked at the driver, and urinated in my shorts. I ran home crying as blood trickled down my legs.

Another refuge of mine was the supermarket on 116th Street. I liked to walk around inside the supermarket and steal sips of soda and bites of candy and fruit. During the summer, crowds of people with radios and coolers and umbrellas poured onto the beach from the 116th Street subway station. These crowds included menacing teenagers. While Paddy and Katie were walking on the boardwalk one day, one of these teenagers pushed Paddy against the railing and started hitting him. Katie panicked and slammed a glass bottle on the teenager's head to set Paddy free.

The courtyard in front of our apartment offered little reprieve from the punks on the beach. The Roche family lived in a neighboring apartment, and they also had a lot of kids—mostly boys. The boys were inclined to bully us when we passed through the courtyard. One of the older boys told me his father beat up my father on the corner of

115th Street the night before. He showed me a big red stain on the sidewalk and claimed it was my father's blood. Katie assured me the stain was merely red paint that had dried on the concrete.

On another day, I came back from the beach and turned into the courtyard to walk toward the stairs that led to our apartment. Some of the Roche family were standing in the courtyard, in front of our stairs, talking to my mother. I walked past everyone and up the stairs. Mickey was looking out of our living room window and onto the courtyard below. He told me he had gotten in a fight with David Roche, our nemesis. David started fights his older brothers finished. During the fight, Mickey grabbed David's hair with both hands and banged his face against the curb, bloodying David's mouth and nose. David's parents had to come out of their apartment to save him.

17

I had many ways to get money for the food that got me through the day—Ring Dings, Hostess CupCakes, Yodels, Chunky Bars, Twinkies, and soda. I colored shells from the beach with crayons and sold them for pennies to people coming out of the subway station. A shoeshine guy who worked near the entrance to the Rockaway Park - 116th Street subway station once let me use his box and supplies to shine shoes. If all else failed, I simply begged. I learned that most people don't want to give money away. Out of frustration in not getting any money from a man coming out of the subway station, I punched him in the stomach. He gave me a hard slap on my face and walked away.

While looking for loose change under washing machines in the laundromat on 116th Street, a lady offered me a job—delivering paper flyers for some sort of election going on at the time. She gave me a large plastic bag of flyers and told me to deliver them on doorsteps and mailboxes all through the area. I spent a few days delivering the flyers, all the while thinking of being paid. I thought I could earn five—or maybe even ten dollars!

At the end of the last day I worked, I noticed a huge crowd had gathered on 116th Street. I couldn't see anything past the swarming mass of grown-ups, so I started pushing my way through, eventually ending up at a stage that was set up in the middle of the street. A man named Nelson

Rockefeller was standing on the stage and talking into a microphone. For a minute, I watched him talk—but then I returned to walking through the crowd, frantically looking for the lady that said she would pay me for delivering the flyers.

18

The Styrofoam surfboard was something anyone could buy for a few dollars at any store near the beach. However, someone had coated it with polyurethane or some other material to make it more rigid. Mickey picked it up from the beach at the end of the day. People were prone to leaving items such as chairs and umbrellas behind as well. He told me I wasn't allowed to use his new possession.

One night, just as dusk was coming on, I snuck the surfboard to the beach and paddled out past the little waves. I eventually got into deep water, about fifty yards from the shore. The only other people in the water were surfers, the nearest one about thirty yards away from me. I became aware of how different the ocean was at dusk. Everything was a wash of pastel colors. The usual airplane and boat sounds were gone. The sound of waves drowned out the distant noise from 116th Street.

I was enjoying this new sense of the beach and lost track of how far I was from the shore. When I realized I was too far out, I tried to paddle back. As I did, the surfboard snapped in half. I slipped into the water and started to sink. Unlike Jamaica Bay, there were no rocks to grab, and dog-paddling back to the shore wasn't an option. I simply accepted I was going to die. I looked up at the surface of the ocean and saw lights flickering from the boardwalk near 116th Street.

The next sensation I felt was the hard grip of a hand on one of my wrists—pulling me up just enough to get my head back into the air. As soon as I took a breath, I realized I had a chance to live again!

I assumed the strong grip on my hand was from a man—but it was just a teenage boy. I instinctively tried to push him down so I could stay up.

"Stop ... stop it ... relax!" he yelled.

I had no control over my body. My instincts said to stay above the water, even if that meant pushing the teenager under the water. He was able to get away from me for a just a moment—long enough for me to understand I had to trust him. When he grabbed me again, I didn't resist. He pulled me toward his surfboard and helped me prop my chest across it. As he paddled us back to the shore, he scolded me for being out in the ocean by myself at night. When my feet hit the sand, I ran straight for the boardwalk—with hot urine running down my legs.

19

It all happened in slow motion. My mother threw a large carving knife out of our living room window and into the courtyard—at my father. I thought about the knife while it was in the air—and about the odds it would hit my father without hurting him. I thought about the handle and the blade as they took turns leading. The odds were good he wouldn't get stabbed—but then I thought about what I had seen on television. Some people *did* get stabbed by knives thrown from far away.

The handle of the knife hit him in the back, and the knife then fell to the concrete near Dennis's feet. Dennis had been standing next to my father.

As a result of this scene, which played out in full view of several neighbors standing in the courtyard, my father moved to a rooming house directly across the street. One afternoon, I went to see him in his basement apartment. I had to walk through his neighbor's apartment to get to it. His neighbor was an obese woman who lived with her son, who was about my age. I hadn't seen the kid in the courtyard or on 115th Street before. The floor in her room was covered with clothes and garbage stacked as high as my waist. As I walked through her apartment, her son sat quietly on a chair in the corner. His mother lay in bed, smoking cigarettes and listening to a small transistor radio.

The "door" to my father's room was a sheet that was attached to a rope with several clothespins. The rope was suspended between two walls. His room was dimly lit by light coming in through a basement window. He seemed to only have a large fan, a radio, and a bed. Wearing his usual street clothes, my father was stretched out on the bed—his head propped up by several pillows. There was no sheet or blanket on the bed. He smoked a Camel cigarette while he read the newspaper.

"Do you live here now, Dad?" I asked.

"Yes, I do. Your momma threw me out."

"Well, when are you coming back?"

"I don't think I'll be coming back."

"Why not?"

"Because your mother has destroyed us all now, son."

20

The only thing that excited me about starting third grade was getting the new black shoes and clip-on ties we needed for assembly day. On some days we didn't go to school—preferring instead to go to our hiding spot under the boardwalk. We used clam shells to dig shallow ditches in the sand. We lay inside our creations and could even fall asleep in them.

When I *did* go to school, I simply went with the flow, walking where other kids walked, doing what they did, all the while desperate to leave. I didn't feel like I belonged in school—and wondered if I was even welcome there. It was a cold and hostile place for me. I did my best to be invisible and stay out of trouble.

My teacher played a game that required half the class to stand on one side of the room and the other half to stand on the other side. She stood in front of the class and asked a kid to read a word on the card she held by her chest. If the kid didn't know the word, they had to sit down. The team with the last player standing won. I never got a word right. I was afraid everyone knew I didn't know how to read—*anything*.

When I told Paddy what was going on in school, he brought two Dr. Seuss books over to me in our living room and patiently taught me how to read them. I could soon read *Green Eggs and Ham* and *The Cat in the Hat* all by myself.

I started reading street signs, store signs, and comic books too. The teacher soon played "the game" again, and I was the last kid standing. She was so excited that she asked the other kids to give me a round of applause.

Paddy also showed me how to multiply numbers by ten.

"Just add zero to the end of any number to get the answer," he said.

"That's so easy," I said.

He told me if I kept adding zeros to the end of the number and didn't stop until the next day, I could get to the biggest number in the universe—infinity!

21

My eighth birthday fell on a cool and sunny October day. I felt safer walking around the streets now, because the crowds that had poured out of the subway station during the summer were now gone. On this day though, my birthday, Katie rounded up my brothers and me from the neighborhood and said we had to take a walk with her and my mother. Katie and my mother, who was crying, walked far ahead of us. We followed them along the boardwalk toward 110th Street, and eventually stopped at the St. John's Home for Boys. On the outside, the home looked like a public school and even had an asphalt playground with basketball courts and high chain-link fences.

We entered through a door on the side of the building, and my brothers and I sat in the waiting room of what seemed to be a church rectory while our mother spoke to the priest in his office—for what felt like an eternity. According to Katie, my mother was looking for a home to place us in—and hoped St. John's could be it. My brothers and I thought living there might not be so bad. We could be around kids like us—and still be near the beach!

My brothers and I eventually got bored and started playing with the water fountain and running around the halls of the rectory to pass the time. Nobody else was there. All the electric lights were off, but sunlight streamed through the windows. St. John's also had a gymnasium, and my brothers and I ran around inside it and tried to make baskets with a basketball that had been lying around. The noise from the bouncing basketball echoed through the building. I wondered how anyone but a full-grown man could score a basket with such a heavy basketball. While we played, Katie stood outside the room where my mother was speaking with the priest.

"What's going on Katie?" Mickey asked.

I added, "Yeah, Katie. What's Mom doing in there with that priest?"

My sister replied, "All I know is Mom said that you guys might have to live here for a while. That's why she was crying. But don't say anything."

"But why?" Paddy wanted to know.

"Mom said we don't have enough money anymore," Katie answered.

I knew we'd been living on some sort of social support because the Roche kids had once reached into our garbage cans and pulled out a clear plastic bag of dried red beans that had been stamped with writing I couldn't read. They said it was "welfare food" and teased us about it.

The door to the priest's office opened ... and I ran straight toward my mother.

"Well, what happened Mom?" I asked.

"Nothing, honey ... nothing."

22

We had to wake up much earlier than usual—so early that it was still dark. Instead of going to school, my parents walked us to the 116th Street subway station to get on the A train. We got off at another station in Jamaica and came out into the sunshine. The November day was unusually nice for New York City. Large orange and red leaves blew across the uneven, cracked sidewalk. Old, decrepit wooden homes lined the street and were occasionally separated by areas where other homes had been razed. The sunlight also illuminated something else: in the commotion of rushing to get on the train, I lost track of where Timmy and Donna were. My parents told us something, but I simply dismissed it along with every other confusing remark that day.

"Where are we going?" Katie wondered.

"Yeah, what's going on?" asked Paddy.

I walked a little faster to get a good look at my parents. I wanted to see their faces straight on when they answered.

My father announced, "You're all going to a party today. There will be a bunch of other kids for you to make friends with. You're all invited."

The situation seemed so strange to me.

We eventually came to an old two-story brick building that was set about 150 feet back from the sidewalk and bordered on the right by a large vacant lot. The building was symmetrical; anyone looking at it from the sky would have seen a squared-off letter C. The walkway led up to the center of the building. The two wings of the building ran parallel to the walkway and toward the street. When we arrived at the front stoop, we saw a tall white man and a skinny black lady waiting at the door. They let us into a small lobby. The man, who wore a dark suit, introduced himself as Mr. Walsh. I thought he looked just like John Wayne.

"Welcome to the Queens Children's Shelter!" he said, bending over to speak with us.

"Everyone just calls it *The Shelter*," the lady said.

None of us said anything back to him. Instead, Mr. Walsh invited my parents into a small office connected to the lobby and closed the door behind them. The rest of us sat on a wooden bench in the lobby, sneaking glances at the lady.

"Where is the party?" Dennis asked her.

"The kids have already left for the party, but you'll get to meet them all later today," she promised.

I questioned, "How many kids are here?"

"Oh my, there's almost a hundred kids here," she declared.

Mickey demanded, "What are *we* doing here?"

Before the lady could answer, my parents exited the office and went straight out the front door without saying goodbye—or even looking at us.

As my parents walked away from the building, Katie continued to gaze through the window until she couldn't see them anymore.

23

The beach near where we once lived on 96th Street looks different. The dusk sky is a bluish purple. The boardwalk and beach come to an absolute stop on 95th Street—where a giant black wall now stands. From a distance, it seems like the wall is made of coal or black marble. It extends well into the ocean and is as high as the Empire State Building.

The ocean suddenly turns from blue to dark green and erupts—its ferocious waves looking to consume me. They roar and crash over the boardwalk, chasing me as I run toward Jamaica Bay. When the waves recede, I go back to the moonlit beach. The water has pooled up into small ponds on the sand, just like it always does after a mad storm. Shopping carts and garbage cans litter the beach, and large sections of the boardwalk are missing or damaged.

I begin searching for my family. I walk from the giant black wall to 115th Street—and then back to the black wall. I eventually find Katie.

"Where is everyone, Katie?"

"I don't know. Maybe they went to Playland ... or maybe they're on the other side of Rockaway Beach Boulevard," she says.

Her answers lack any sense of urgency or alarm.

"Or maybe they're at that bar where Dad goes on 110th Street, you know? The one he dragged the thirty-three-pound striped bass into?" she wonders aloud.

"C'mon, Katie! Where is everyone?" I scream.

"I don't know, Kevin."

We continue walking together along the darkened beach and finally find my mother. The three of us go looking for the rest of our family, but we lose Katie during the search. My mother and I then find Mickey, but then we lose our mother. I eventually wind up near the giant black wall again—alone.

24

The lady brought each of us two pairs of blue socks. She said she was going to show us the building and where our beds were. I had no idea what was going on. A black teenager named Anastasia, who was heavyset and wore her hair straightened out and combed to one side of her head, took Katie to the left wing of the building, which housed all the girls. The right wing was where the boys stayed. Within an hour or so, we knew the junior boys, who were eight years old or less, lived on the first floor—in the front of the wing. The intermediate boys, who were nine and ten years old, also lived on the first floor, but in the rear of the building. The senior boys, who were older than ten, had the whole second floor to themselves. The girls' wing used an identical layout.

Dennis and I were junior boys. We were less than a year apart in age, and except for the fact that I was an inch taller than him, we were practically clones. We both had green eyes, brown hair, and fish-belly-white skin. Our room contained about fifteen single beds that were each lined up perpendicular to a wall. A small nightstand separated each bed from the next. Opposite our beds was a row of windows that allowed us to look down onto the center sidewalk that led to the entrance of the building.

Mickey was an intermediate boy and stayed in a similar room across the hall near the rear of the building.

His room had just a few windows that faced the rear of the building. Paddy stayed with the senior boys on the second floor. Katie was a senior girl and went to the second floor of the girls' wing.

After seeing our respective rooms, we were led into the cafeteria, which contained dozens of folding tables and chairs set in rows. A soda machine stood across the hall from the entrance to the cafeteria. We then toured the basement, which had several classrooms and a shop room with a bunch of big machines in it. We were then led to the back of the building to view a playground with swings, monkey bars, and a baseball diamond painted onto the blacktop.

A waist-high chain-link fence separated the playground from a decrepit wooden house. Although the house looked abandoned, a little black girl, maybe four years old, ran out of the house and up to the fence to say hello to us. Wearing a coat, she was barefoot and naked from the waist down. I was stunned by her appearance. I saw dried dirt on her skinny little legs. I now knew *I* wasn't poor.

We then went back into the cafeteria and sat down, waiting for the other kids to return. The tables were still in rows, but quarts of milk had been placed on top of them at regular intervals. Gold and yellow streamers and paper turkeys decorated the room for Thanksgiving. While we waited, Paddy started to drink directly from one of the quarts of milk.

A young black woman standing near the entrance to the cafeteria shouted, "Don't you dare put your mouth on that milk, young man!"

We were all frightened to be yelled at from a voice that seemed to come out of nowhere.

THE RIVER

She rushed over to our table and crouched down to talk to Paddy. In a stern tone, the woman instructed, "Honey, that milk is for sharing. We pass the container around here, and everyone gets to pour their own milk into their *own* glass. We never put our mouths on the container. Got it?"

25

The kids showed up in waves. Most were black, some were Puerto Rican, and a few others were white—little kids and big kids, girls and boys, all noisy as hell. None of them paid any attention to us. They lined up and got trays and then headed into a little area where food was handed out, just like in a school lunchroom. My brothers and I followed them through the line and came back to our table only to realize our seats had been taken. At the very moment when I absolutely needed my brothers, I couldn't be near them. Dennis and I had to sit with the junior boys. Katie refused to come into the cafeteria and scurried off into the kitchen area instead. Mr. Walsh allowed her to stay in the kitchen, where she made herself a peanut butter and jelly sandwich.

As Dennis and I ate, I noticed almost all the counselors at The Shelter were black. The girls were supervised by a rotund lady named Mrs. Tripp, a short and stocky older lady named Mrs. Stevens, and Anastasia. The kids sitting nearby knew we were new arrivals and started talking to us.

"Where are you from?"

"Rockaway," I replied. After a moment, I asked, "Do you live here?"

"No!" yelled one of the kids.

"Nobody *lives* here!" laughed another.

THE RIVER

"We just stay here until we get to go back home," a senior boy explained. "Don't worry though. You're going to see your parents again. Parents come back here on visiting Sunday."

Yet another kid assured us, "Yeah, you're going to see them. They'll come back."

26

Evidently, Monday night was "fight night." The counselors wanted everyone to know how to fight. This scared the hell out of me. I didn't know how to fight, and I was certain every kid there could kick my ass. I wondered how much fighting would go on at The Shelter. I wasn't sure whether anyone there would come to my aid if I was getting beaten up.

The counselors came to our room and told all of us to go to the largest classroom in the basement. The desks and chairs were stacked in the back, and wrestling mats were placed on the floor. While everyone stood at the perimeter of the room, the counselors called out two names at a time and helped the corresponding boys put on boxing gloves. The counselors then positioned the boys in the middle of the makeshift ring. I watched a whole bunch of fights. Most of them involved wild flailing and an occasional direct hit to the face or head that made everyone in the room start screaming and laughing. The counselors acted like coaches, yelling at the kids as they fought.

"C'mon now ... stay in there!"

"Keep your hands up!"

"Punch ... punch!"

If the fight got out of control, the counselors stopped it.

"Good job ... good job!"

Plenty of advice was given to the kids, who probably didn't hear a word.

"Next time, keep your hands up, and you won't get hit so much."

"Stick your jab out more!"

"Proud of you guys!"

"Now, let's get those gloves off and shake hands, alright?"

All the other kids had to clap. On that first night, I started to worry they might call my name.

Someone yelled out, "Kevin and Lloyd … Kevin and Lloyd … come on out here!"

A counselor kneeled and helped me put on a pair of eggplant-colored plastic boxing gloves. Lloyd was a stocky little black kid—like a miniature Joe Frazier! I knew right away he had already been boxing at The Shelter. He kept jabbing my face, and the seams on his gloves left thin cuts that burned as my sweat leaked into them. A counselor yelled advice and directions at me, but I was dealing with Lloyd at the time and didn't hear a word. I really didn't care that Lloyd beat me. I felt as though I was now part of the group. After that night, Lloyd and I still saw each other from time to time, but we hardly spoke. Kids were always coming into and leaving The Shelter. Most stayed for only a few weeks.

My next fight was against a Puerto Rican kid who was my height and skinny just like me. He was active and flashy with his hands, and although he didn't wallop me as badly as Lloyd did, he hit my face and abdomen with many light shots. He clearly won. I asked him to teach me to fight like that, and he did. I used his style of boxing for the rest of my fights there, some of which I may have won.

27

None of the classrooms in the basement had windows. My class had about thirty kids in it. My teacher was a young white lady with brunette hair and glasses. She was friendly—but stern when she had to be. A boy who sat next to me liked to masturbate while she talked. She scolded him a few times, and made the girls sit on the other side of the room.

When she spoke, I tuned the rest of the world out. She seemed to hypnotize me—everything she said went straight into my brain. She used M&Ms to teach us how to multiply and divide. She taught us about Lapland and the Sámi people. She showed us a film about Pablo Picasso—twice. She made us write down whatever she wrote on the blackboard. One major assignment was about the Great Chicago Fire. She wrote paragraph after paragraph, for days and days, all about the fire. On one day, we had to write in script; on the next day, we had to write in printed letters. She also called on each one of us to read in front of the class.

In a lesson that lasted weeks, we had to memorize a map of South America. We each had to pick a country, draw its map, and write a report about it. Every report had to share one interesting fact about the country and name its capital. I chose Chile because of its unusual map, and I talked about how it had the ocean on one side and mountains on the other.

The teacher set up our seats in rows—like we were sitting in an airplane. She was the captain of the airplane.

"We are now flying over Brazil!" she said.

This prompted the kid who picked Brazil to stand up, show his map, name the capital, and state an interesting fact about Brazil. And then we were on to another country.

The basement also contained a dark, hot shop room. The old white man who ran it showed us how to make rubber stamps with our names on them; how to melt glass for decorative enamel pins; and how to align printing letters into a chuck and use it for printing. Additional arts and crafts activities took place in the cafeteria. Among other skills, I learned how to sew by hand and how to use a sewing machine. After a couple of months, I looked like a genius compared to the kids who just arrived.

Mrs. Stevens was the music teacher. She was chubby and had hair like James Brown's—straightened out like a white person's and curled underneath. She wore fake eyelashes and lots of lipstick. The music room was a small room just outside the cafeteria—with just enough space for a stand-up piano and several chairs. Mrs. Stevens asked groups of five or six kids to sit as close to her as possible while she played the piano and sang. The songs were gospel songs such as "Michael Row Your Boat Ashore"; Christmas songs such as "Jingle Bell Rock" and "Silent Night"; and basic kids' songs such as "Old MacDonald Had a Farm."

As she turned the pages of sheet music, I noticed the tips of her fingers were bent sideways. I also watched her feet hit the pedals, and I wondered how she could possibly know which pedal to step on while playing piano with her fingers and singing at the same time. Her stockings had so many runs in them—but she didn't seem to care!

She wanted to hear us sing every song. She looked at me with her big eyes and big eyelashes and knew I wasn't singing—I was just moving my lips.

"Come on now—you can do this!" she cheered.

Eventually, I found the courage to blow just a faint sound from my mouth. I listened and looked around, expecting someone to make fun of me. When that didn't happen, I released more sound. I gradually learned to trust the other kids. I sang out loud just like they did.

28

The two shower rooms were about twelve feet by twelve feet and boasted numerous overhead spouts. The floors, walls, and ceilings were covered with little blue and white tiles arranged in a checkered pattern. There was only one way in or out of the shower—a narrow door-like opening that sat on a step that kept the water inside.

The junior boys showered at night. We all went in together—naked. A counselor named Mr. Jones went in with us. He was a short, bald black man, and he was also naked. We were all shocked at the size of his penis, which seemed to be erect most of the time. We giggled and tried not to look at it or let him hear us laughing. He stroked himself while he talked to us about how to clean ourselves. I just kept my back to everyone and faced the wall until I could get out of there. Before we were allowed to leave, Mr. Jones stood by the door and checked everyone's penises and asses, to see if we cleaned them.

"Hold your hands up over your head now."

"Let me see what you got."

"Uh huh, hmm ...." he said, as he moved my penis from one side to the other and spread my ass cheeks to steal a look.

Then, I'd be free to go.

29

On Christmas Eve, we ate a turkey dinner while Mrs. Stevens played "Jingle Bell Rock" on a piano that was set up in the front of the cafeteria. The atmosphere was fun and festive. Afterward, the counselors split us up into groups of ten to fifteen kids and marched us through the falling snow. We visited a bunch of group homes that had older kids living in them. The homes were dilapidated wooden houses.

Groups of kids sat on couches and bunk beds that were set up in living rooms. The floors in some of the houses were so slanted they reminded me of Playland's playhouse. The older kids and counselors sang Christmas songs and hugged each other—and me too. There was so much joy in the air. I loved that Santa Claus was black!

When we got back to The Shelter, we went straight to our rooms and lay in bed. Dennis and I and a couple of other kids got up later in the night and looked out the windows of our room, up into the sky, and watched the snow fall. A couple of younger kids asked me if Santa Claus was real.

I informed them, "Me and my brothers and sister waited up the whole night one time, but he never came. So, there is no *real* Santa Claus—they're all fake! It's just old guys who wear Santa Claus suits. I even saw them tonight.

My mother even told us there was no such thing as Santa Claus. Ain't I right, Dennis?"

"No, she didn't," Dennis insisted. "There *is* a Santa Claus! And those guys who wear the suits are Santa Claus's helpers."

"Oh my God, Dennis—you're just like a baby! How can you believe in Santa Claus?" I taunted.

"I just know he's real, that's all," he replied. "You'll see."

We were up later than we ever had been before, and I wondered whether we'd reached midnight. If midnight had arrived, then Christmas had as well. As I watched the snow fall, I saw two adults and a child walk toward the front door. I thought they were just coming back late from one of the parties. A short time later, a counselor brought a little black kid into our darkened room.

"Can you boys talk to Tyrone, our new boy?" the counselor asked.

"Sure—we'll talk to him!"

The counselor gave Tyrone a nudge toward us and then left. Tyrone didn't take another step. He seemed to be my age and had big eyes and long eyelashes and protruding teeth. He wouldn't stop crying or take his thumb out of his mouth, and his nose was running. He wasn't wearing socks, and his oversized sneakers didn't even have laces. Tyrone was poor—just like the little girl I had seen by the fence. He was shaking and couldn't catch his breath. We tried to console him.

"Don't be afraid, Tyrone—it's fun here!"

"We'll be your friends, Tyrone."

I put my arm around his back. I didn't know what to say. It didn't matter—the other boys were talking to him.

Later that night, likely near two o'clock in the morning, we took him into the bathroom and combed his hair with Vaseline—something both white and black kids loved to do at The Shelter. He watched in the mirror while we parted and slicked back his hair with Vaseline. Even though he was sucking his thumb, I saw a smile sneak onto his face a few times. As he calmed down, we talked to him about Christmas.

"Hey Tyrone, we're all gonna get presents tomorrow," Dennis said.

"Yeah, even you, Tyrone," I agreed.

Tyrone started talking to us.

"Uh huh" for yes.

"Uh uh" for no.

His thumb never left his mouth. I noticed Tyrone's ankles and shins had some sort of white flaky stuff on them. I had seen it before on some other kids.

"The counselor's gonna spray some stuff on your legs tomorrow," I told him.

30

Christmas Day was clear and cold. The counselors led one group of kids at a time toward a large military-looking tent set up behind The Shelter. As we walked, wind blew plumes of snow into my face. After entering the tent, we walked down a central aisle flanked on both sides by rows of metal shelving. Each row had a piece of yellow masking tape on it labelled with a black crayon—indicating the specific group of kids that should stop there. The words "Junior Boys" showed up on a few shelves to our right, halfway down the central aisle.

"Grab five presents and five presents only!" the counselors yelled.

The excitement was almost too much for me. Some kids scrambled for the biggest presents. I grabbed five random ones and tried to catch my breath. After we obtained our loot, we went back inside The Shelter and ripped into whatever presents we hadn't opened on the walk back. The presents I opened were previously owned items: a small plastic football, a checkers game, and three puzzles.

The excitement of Christmas affected everyone, causing The Shelter to fall into a chaotic state. Counselors struggled to help parents and kids find one another. Parents and counselors stepped over wrapping paper and kids who were opening their gifts in the hallways and stairwells.

We hadn't seen our parents since the day they dropped us off at The Shelter. I frantically ran through the crowded halls looking for them, trying all the while not to drop any of my presents. I soon found them standing in the lobby with Katie and Paddy. I immediately noticed Donna and Timmy weren't with them. I also noticed something was wrong with my mother. She was crying—and her eyes were blinking fast. As I hugged her, she looked down and away from me. She was crying too hard to hug me back. I could smell alcohol and cigarettes on her breath. That was my mother's smell—and it comforted me. I tried to talk with her, but she could only look back at me for a moment and nod. I thought she was lost in her mind and couldn't get out.

31

Mrs. Tripp acted like a school principal, keeping the place in line by yelling a steady cadence of orders at counselors and kids. I wasn't afraid of her—I did whatever she told me to. She was generous with hugs and had a gentle voice in one-on-one situations. Mr. Blake was friendly and wore nice suits. He parked his big purple Cadillac Coupe de Ville, which had wings on the back, in the playground for everyone to marvel at. Mrs. Tripp and Mr. Blake liked to walk together and joke around as they ran the place.

There was also a thin black lady who pushed a broom or a mop around. She seemed to show up at random times and places within The Shelter. She hardly spoke to us but always had a smile. She wore a light blue dress with a white belt and white shoes that had a lot of scuff marks on them.

We also had a tall black guy with a big belly who woke us up every morning.

"Rise and shine! Rise and Shine!" he yelled as he cracked a bull whip on the floor.

He was not afraid to use the whip around kids. He once hit Tyrone near the groin with it, "by accident." We all woke up when we heard the rise-and-shine routine kick in—every time.

After my first six months at The Shelter, the counselors decided I should be "moved up" from the junior boys to be the leader of the intermediate boys. In effect, I moved from a bed at the front of the building to a bed at the back of the building. Dennis stayed with the junior boys and Mickey got bumped up to the senior boys. As leader, I had to make sure all the kids made their beds before we went to breakfast. To motivate us to complete the chore properly, the guy with the whip came by and tried to bounce a quarter off each bed.

"If it bounces on your bed, then you made your bed just like a soldier," he claimed.

The quarter never bounced.

The only time a bed didn't need to be made was when a kid had peed in it. Checking on that was my job. When a kid wet his bed, I told him to throw the sheets or blankets down the laundry chute in the hall. I then made sure he replaced the soiled sheets or blankets with clean ones. I wet the bed on many nights, so it really didn't matter to me.

In addition to the big guy with the whip, there was an old white guy who mopped the floors with a cleaning agent that smelled like Clorox. He was about fifty years old and didn't talk much. He was obsessed with preventing us from getting and spreading athlete's foot and made sure we wore our flip-flops when we walked in and out of the bathroom. He even sprayed kids' feet and ankles with chemicals if he thought they had athlete's foot.

One morning, well before the time to get up for breakfast, he roused me from my bed. The sky outside was still quite dark, and I was in a daze. He led me to the back of The Shelter, where his rusty old green pickup truck was parked. He had to help me get into the truck because the passenger door was heavy and the handle was broken.

THE RIVER

"I'm gonna need your help today," he declared, lighting up a cigarette.

"OK," I replied.

He drove to the backs of restaurants, delicatessens, and diners—places he apparently knew of from prior trips. He parked the truck near the dumpsters and used a flashlight to look for bread, rolls, and donuts. My job was to jump into the dumpsters and throw the food into large brown paper bags. The bags had clearly been used many times before. I climbed over cardboard boxes, slimy food, rags, bottles, and newspapers to get to the donuts and bread. He spoke to me as I trampled through the dumpster.

"I've been doing this for quite a while, kiddo," he stated.

"Uh huh," I agreed.

"Heinz used to help me with this. Do you know Heinz?"

"Yeah, I know him. He's a senior boy with my brother Paddy."

"Well, Heinz ain't here no more."

"Oh, OK," I said.

"The other kids don't need to know about this, alright?"

"Don't worry, I won't tell."

32

I waited in a long line that led to the laundry room. As I waited, I saw one kid at a time come out wearing new sneakers. The kids screamed with excitement and ran to the playground. When I finally got inside, some lady measured my shoe size. Within minutes, she brought me a pair of green high-top PF Flyer sneakers. The first thing I did after putting them on was what every other kid did that day—run around the playground. I could tell right away those green PF Flyers made me run faster. In my mind, I was the fastest kid on the playground. I couldn't wait to put those sneakers on each morning. In addition to the playground, the counselors liked to set us free in a nearby park called Forest Park. With my new PF Flyers, I ran through trails and woods at full speed. I was almost flying.

On Tuesday nights, the counselors walked us to a YMCA that was about a mile from The Shelter. We had to shower before being admitted to the pool area, where swimming coaches waited for us. They instructed us to get into the pool and grab onto the sides. I don't think anyone knew how to swim, but we were told to kick our legs for extended periods, maybe five minutes at most, with the intent of getting the water splashy. The coaches then had us try to swim in the shallow end, from one side to the other. Each swimmer tagged someone to take the next turn. This went on for a few weeks before we were asked to do the same in the deep end. Some of us picked up the skill and were soon jumping off the diving board, cruising underneath the water, and having a blast. After my two near drownings, it felt good to know I had finally learned to swim.

The Shelter also sent me away to Pythian Camp for two weeks. We took a bus from the Port Authority Bus Station in Manhattan to a town in Upstate New York called Glen Spey. There were many small cabins, clustered in groups of three or four, and spread out over acres of forest and streams. Seven other kids stayed in my cabin, and the camp counselors kept us busy with all sorts of activities and long walks in the woods. I even got to see deer! We collected bugs and butterflies and fossils. At night, we had campfires and told stories. Pythian Camp also had a small movie theater that played cartoons.

I wrote a postcard to Katie at The Shelter's address, telling her I loved being at camp but was "coming home" soon. When I got back, I realized there was "a thing" going on at The Shelter: everyone was getting a girlfriend.

"I hate girls! I hate girls! I hate girls!" I yelled as I ran around the playground.

I yelled until my voice went hoarse—but it didn't matter. Several kids formed a circle by locking arms and several other kids corralled me inside the circle with a skinny blonde girl named Mary Ellen Naismith. With the encouragement of the kids around us, Mary Ellen and I kissed each other "on the lips." Our kiss lasted about a fraction of a second, but it was a done deal. Mary Ellen and I were officially hooked up. She left The Shelter a few weeks later.

33

My mother eventually got well again, at least well enough to visit us on visiting Sundays. In fact, my parents could even take us away for the day—as long as we returned before it got dark. They had an apartment in the basement of a yellow house in Jackson Heights. The apartment was just a few houses away from the subway station at 74th Street and Roosevelt Avenue. The neighborhood was loaded with Irish Bars with names like The Liffey, Davitt's & McDonough, The Shamrock, Patrick's, and The Ready Penny.

My first visit to the apartment was on Easter Sunday. I was surprised to see it was a nice apartment, and I thought if they could afford *this* place, they might be rich enough to take us all back home. On their bedroom dresser was a plastic model of a ship called the *H.M.S. Bounty*. My father had assembled it by gluing a bunch of little parts together and tying tiny knots to secure the sails. In the top drawer of the dresser was a white athletic sock filled with quarters. It seemed like a fortune to me.

"We're saving so we can get you kids back home," my father explained.

"Wow, can I hold it?" I asked.

After gaining permission, I lifted the sock overhead with both hands, wondering aloud, "How much money *is* this?"

THE RIVER

"That's about three hundred dollars!" my father boasted.

"Wow!" Dennis exclaimed. "Let me hold it!"

While my brother took his turn, I examined the sheets of little green stamps sitting on top of the dresser.

My father announced, "We're in the Irish Sweepstakes, too, son—it's the Irish lottery. We'll be rich if we win, and we'll have you all back home in no time if we do."

"Where are Donna and Timmy now, Mom?" I asked.

"Yeah, where *are* they?" Mickey echoed.

"They're in a foster home in Brooklyn," she admitted.

"Don't worry, Kevin," my father declared. "We'll get them back too."

During one of my visits to Jackson Heights, my parents bought me a small cactus plant. The cactus plant was about four inches tall and sat in a clay pot about the size of my fist. The man at the plant store told me it was a "prickly pear" cactus and a yellow flower would grow out of it one day. I took it back to The Shelter and watered it every week. I could see little buds growing out of it and I wondered how big it would be by the time my family got back together again. I liked to show the plant to other kids—and I sometimes carried it to the playground or my classroom.

While walking down a set of stairs to my classroom, the little clay pot slipped out of my hands and fell to the base of the stairs. The pot cracked into several pieces and spilled the plant and soil onto the floor. I frantically tried to save the plant by placing it in a glass jar and adding some dirt from the playground. It died in just a day or two.

The loss of my cactus plant caused me to cry uncontrollably. The outburst was enough to get the attention of Anastasia, who was in the basement laundry room with Mrs. Tripp. She was putting nail polish on Mrs. Tripp's toenails, who was sitting on a big wooden chair. Anastasia tried to console me by telling me she had a secret that would make me happy.

"You Weadocks have been here long enough," she declared. "You're gonna be leaving here soon."

I was so excited that I started jumping and screaming, "I'm going home! I'm going back home!"

"No, no, no!" she interrupted. "You're going to Little Flower."

When Labor Day weekend came, my siblings and I hugged the counselors and got into a station wagon idling behind The Shelter. I was surprised to see Anastasia cry.

34

After a long drive on many highways, we got off an exit that led to a town on the north shore of Long Island called Wading River. The road we got on had nothing but sod farms on both sides. After a few miles, we came to a stop sign, at which we could only make a left or a right. A bunch of little signs on a white wooden post pointed in different directions and displayed various names of things and places nearby. The little sign for Little Flower directed us to the left. We drove up a long hill, and after about a mile, we saw a white fence on our left side.

"This is the fence. We must be here," said the counselor who was driving the station wagon.

The white fence was about a mile long and about six feet tall. Dense woods crowded the space behind it. We turned left at the entrance gate and then drove down a long road that took us through the woods. A football field eventually appeared on our right side. A couple hundred yards later, we parked outside the administration building, which was also on the right. The building was next to a pond that was about an acre in size. The pond was surrounded by trees and filled with water lilies, frogs, and fish. A dirt footpath wound around the water's edge.

Across the road, about one hundred yards away from the pond, were four brick bungalows. A school stood to the left of the bungalows, and a separate gymnasium building stood behind the school. Several acres of lawn, including a baseball field, spanned from the right side of the gym to the tall woods in the distance.

Little Flower seemed to have been built around a church at the center of the campus. The church was the most prominent building there. It had stained glass and wooden pews that one might expect in a well-appointed church in an upscale community.

The Long Island Sound was less than two hundred yards away and accessible through a small break in the woods behind the bungalows. About twenty yards into the break, a set of white wooden stairs zigzagged down a cliff to the beach below. The woods created a tight canopy over the stairs, shading most of the descent. The smell of the ocean air was everywhere.

Little Flower was much quieter and less crowded than The Shelter. We were also isolated from the rest of the world by the Long Island Sound in one direction and miles of woods around us. Only the long driveway connected us to the nearest public road.

In addition to its natural beauty, Little Flower featured two Irish Wolfhounds that lumbered across the campus during the day. The dogs were massive—their heads level with my own. They had huge teeth and dark gray hair that was long and wiry. One was named Brian, and the other was named Sean—a fun fact for Dennis and me because his middle name was Brian, and mine was Shaun. The dogs were like no other dogs we had ever seen! They seemed like magical beasts to us, and I was lucky enough to have them walk toward me once. Fearing they might change their mind and walk in a different direction, I made sure to stand still until they were close enough to pet.

35

Katie, Paddy, and Mickey were placed in foster homes within a few days of our arrival. Katie went to live with the Whitcomb family out in Southampton, a coastal town on the east end of Long Island. Paddy and Mickey went to live with the Kowalski family in Bohemia, also on the eastern side of Long Island.

Just Dennis and I remained at Little Flower. We lived in the San Juan cottage. It was a nice, modern, single-story building, and each of us stayed in a room with three other kids. In total, sixteen kids lived in San Juan cottage, which had a huge clean kitchen with two refrigerators and an island counter with stools. The living room had three or four sofas clustered around the large black-and-white TV on a stand in the corner.

The person in charge of Little Flower was a middle-aged white priest named Father Fagan, and he lived in a brick house that was tucked in the woods—close to a cliff that overlooked the Sound. Each cottage was supervised by a live-in nun. The nuns wore long white robes with blue trim and they spoke Polish as their first language. Our nun was Sister Lawrence, a woman of few words who didn't hug us like the black ladies did at The Shelter. She wore glasses and had wrinkly pale skin. In addition to nuns, Little Flower had counselors who showed up on weekends.

We met the main counselor on the first weekend we were there. He was a young white guy with an athletic build and black hair. He told jokes and kidded around with us and was full of positive energy. He served us uncut personal-size pizza pies for dinner. He wanted to take us to the beach before dark, so we carried our pizzas outside and headed toward the cliff. Dusk was setting in as we descended via the zigzag stairs, which were really kind of intimidating at first. I began to think and hope Little Flower was going to be a great place to live, like The Shelter was.

When we finally reached the beach, some kids flung what was left of their pizzas onto the sand or at each other. The beach was private, and we were the only people around for as far as I could see. I took off my sneakers and walked out into the Sound until the clear, cold water reached my knees. I noticed the Sound was very different from the ocean at Rockaway Beach. In the ocean, particularly at high tide, the water level could be over my head within just twenty feet of the shore. In the Sound, no waves disturbed the surface, and I'd have to go out about thirty feet farther to be totally submerged. Unlike Rockaway Beach, the bottom of the Sound wasn't smooth and sandy; it was rocky. Most of the rocks were as big as baseballs—others were the size of washing machines and refrigerators.

The business of getting our First Holy Communion was set in motion a week or two after we arrived. The nuns rounded up all the stragglers who hadn't received Holy Communion yet and got them ready for the big day at the church. Dennis and I had been baptized at The Shelter earlier in the same year. It was a *big* day for everyone at Little Flower, and we had to make sure we could recite the Our Father and Hail Mary prayers.

THE RIVER

After my Communion, I was eligible to go to confessions on each Saturday. I didn't really know what to tell Father Fagan, who sat on the other side of the wall. Every time I went in, I said the same thing: I cursed a lot, and I was mean to Dennis. I received three Our Fathers and a Hail Mary as my penance and was on my way out to the pews. I felt better after saying those prayers. My soul was clean. For the time being, I wasn't going to hell. The other kids and I talked about mortal sins and regular sins and the fact that regular sins left white spots on the soul which went away after confession. The mortal sins—such as murder and not believing in God—left permanent black spots. Having a lot of regular sins put you in purgatory for a long time, and then you still had to hope to get to heaven. Having just one mortal sin meant you went to hell forever.

Our school at Little Flower looked like a smaller version of a regular suburban school. The single-story building was made up of red bricks and contained hallways, a principal's office, and classrooms that had plenty of windows. The classrooms were small, about twelve feet by twenty feet, with desks jammed in so tightly that walking around them was difficult. I spent much of the day dozing off or looking out the windows. The school day was short and ended right after lunch with an hour of recess. We spent that hour watching television while the teachers talked and smoked cigarettes in an adjacent room.

36

Just like at The Shelter, visits from our parents were on the third Sunday of every month. One of the big differences was that we were about fifty miles from the city, which meant my parents needed a car. Another big difference was that only Dennis and I lived at Little Flower. The rest of my siblings had to be brought there by their respective foster parents. Yet another difference was that only one of my parents showed up on each visiting Sunday—my mother on one visiting Sunday and my father on the next.

When my mother showed up, we went to a little café near San Juan cottage. The café was small, about fifteen feet by twenty feet, and sold snacks, coffee, and hot chocolate. There was a small ice cream box as well, the kind with sliding glass doors on the top that needed to be pushed aside before we could reach for the ice cream. Two or three round tables dotted the café, but they were small and intended for couples. Because the café was crowded on visiting Sundays, we were usually left standing.

I was an emotional volcano on the days my mother visited us. I cried easily—but then felt joy because we were all together again—and then I went back to crying. I clung to my mother—and the familiar smell of cigarettes and alcohol on her breath. On one visiting Sunday, Donna and Timmy were also there. I hadn't seen them in a year. Donna was five years old, and Timmy was three. They barely said anything to me. All they wanted to do was hug my mother's leg. Both had runny noses and facial bruises, and Donna had large patches of hair missing from her head. My mother spent most of that visit crying and shaking, just like she did on Christmas Day at The Shelter.

37

I began to realize Little Flower was not like The Shelter, where kids were held until their family situations straightened out. At Little Flower, the hope of going back to one's own family was lost. It was merely a holding tank for kids waiting to be placed into foster homes.

On Thanksgiving Day, Dennis and I were driven out to the foster home where Paddy and Mickey lived. We arrived and were introduced to the Kowalski family and then escorted around the house by Paddy and Mickey, who were excited to show us their room and the backyard. To me, those people were rich—their house had four bedrooms! My brothers seemed happy there, but later in the day, Paddy told me he felt like Mrs. Kowalski treated her own boys better than she treated him and Mickey.

During Thanksgiving dinner, I noticed the plates and cups and bowls seemed very fancy, with lots of intricate designs painted on them. I read on the bottom of my cup that it was made in England.

"Are all of you guys from England?" I wondered aloud.

As the Kowalski family giggled, Paddy looked at me like I was crazy.

Mrs. Kowalski asked, "So, Kevin, how do you like living at Little Flower?"

"It's fun," I replied.

"And Dennis, how about you? Do you like living there, too?"

"Yeah, I guess," Dennis muttered.

Mrs. Kowalski continued with her questions for a while, and we continued with our brief responses.

"And who actually stays with you in the bungalow? The nuns? The counselors?"

"The nuns—but our nun is mean!" I exclaimed, smiling at my brothers.

"Oh, she is, is she?" prodded Mrs. Kowalski.

I agreed, "Yeah, Sister Lawrence is always mad at us and never talks to us."

Dennis and I slept over at the Kowalskis' that night, and said goodbye to our brothers in the morning. A social worker drove us back to Little Flower in a station wagon. Sister Lawrence stood outside San Juan cottage waiting for us to get out of the car. I could tell right away she was furious about something. She immediately grabbed my ear and pulled me into my room.

"So, I'm mean lady?" she yelled. "Why I'm mean lady? Why? You're bad! I don't want you here!"

Sister Lawrence refused to look at me or talk to me anymore. She terrified me. Within a week, she told Dennis and me to sit at the island counter in the kitchen and wait for her. She showed up about an hour later and informed us, "You're going to foster home tomorrow. Go to bed."

The next day was one of those cloudy and cold days that fall between Thanksgiving and Christmas. Sister Lawrence put her hand on my back and nudged me out of San Juan cottage and into the back seat of a station wagon driven by a thin, white, middle-aged man in an off-white trench coat. His name was Mr. Dewey. There were no goodbyes to the other kids in our bungalow. Our parents weren't around to explain anything to us. Dennis and I timidly asked Mr. Dewey a bunch of questions, starting with, "Where are we going?"

"You're going to your *own* foster home now," Mr. Dewey answered, looking at us in the rearview mirror as he drove. "It's a nice place, and the parents are nice, too. They have another boy living there right now, and they have their own son, too."

"How long does it take to get there?" I inquired.

"You'll be there in no time, maybe a half-hour."

I continued, "Do our parents know we're going there?"

"Of course they do! You'll still see them on visiting Sundays at Little Flower," he assured us.

We were soon off the highway and driving through a town called Farmingville. We parked in the driveway of a house on a street called Waverly Avenue.

38

The house was a small ranch, maybe 1,200 square feet at most, without a garage or carport. The foster parents were standing on the walkway that led from the driveway to the front stoop. I took a few steps out of the car and stopped—waiting for Mr. Dewey to start the conversation. I looked at the foster parents long enough to see the father was tall and the mother was short, fat, and ugly. Her bleached blonde hair had an inch or two of black roots and didn't seem to have been combed or brushed at all. She stared oddly, as though looking past me. Her eyes were stretched wide open, and the half-smile on her face seemed forced. Both seemed to be in their thirties. We followed them up the two or three stairs of the stoop and into their house. A small black Lab named Queenie gave us a friendly greeting as we stepped into the living room.

Mr. Dewey spoke to the foster parents while Dennis and I stood apart from them and pet Queenie. We were waiting for whatever was going to happen next. Mr. Dewey eventually said goodbye to us and walked out of the house. My heart started pounding the moment the door closed behind him. At The Shelter and Little Flower, I could mix in with groups of kids to distance myself from bullies or weirdos. Now there was no place to hide.

The foster parents told us their names were Isaac and Nellie Waterman.

"Well, it's nice to meet you, Kevin and Dennis. We've heard so much about you."

"Thank you," we muttered.

"We've set up a room for you to share together," Isaac Waterman announced. "It's your own bedroom."

Nellie Waterman chirped, "You can call us Aunt Nellie and Uncle Isaac—if you want."

"Or Mom and Dad, if that sounds better to you," Isaac Waterman suggested.

I was repulsed by the very thought of calling them Mom and Dad. I was also shocked to think this was where we were in our lives—possibly having to call these strangers Mom and Dad! I wondered whether my mother and father were aware of what was happening to us.

"Aunt and uncle," I mumbled, staring at the floor.

Dennis agreed, "Yeah, aunt and uncle are good."

"How old are you Kevin?" asked Nellie Waterman.

"Nine."

"And how about you, Dennis?"

"I'm eight."

"So, I don't know if you already know this, but we have been foster parents for many years," boasted Nellie Waterman. "The boy and girl who left a few months ago are still writing us letters."

"Every kid who ever lived with us loved it here," Isaac Waterman declared in a matter-of-fact way as he packed some tobacco into his pipe.

They then introduced us to a fourteen-year-old Spanish boy named Carlos. He shared the front bedroom with Anthony, the Watermans' three-year-old biological son. Anthony slept in a small bed just a few feet from Carlos' bed.

THE RIVER

Our small bedroom had a closet, two little windows, and two single beds, one on each wall. My bed was against the wall that was shared with the master bedroom. I immediately noticed our room smelled like piss.

Moments after Dennis and I went into our room, Carlos came in to talk to us. He was almost the size of a man—and wore a white T-shirt that revealed real muscles on his arms. I could tell by the way he talked he was a tough kid. I had been around a lot of them in The Shelter, and Carlos was no different. I wasn't afraid of him; I sensed he wanted nothing to do with us.

"I've been here for over a year," Carlos stated.

He spoke in a low but confident voice.

"That Waterman man is a motherfucker. I don't take shit from him or his fat-ass wife. I heard what they told you kids—that's all bullshit! They're both motherfuckers. They fucked those other little kids up bad, man. They was lucky to get the fuck out of here. Don't believe *anything* they say to you, man. They're lying motherfuckers. They're gonna get rid of my ass soon though. I can't wait. I hate that motherfucker Isaac. I tried stabbing his ass, but I missed. He don't fuck with me no more. Ain't no knives in this house now, man!"

Dennis and I thought Carlos was a little crazy, so we weren't sure if we should believe *anything* he said. We chose to laugh instead—like he was putting on a show for us. Carlos didn't talk to us much after that, and after a week, he was indeed gone.

39

My first day of fourth grade at Waverly Avenue Elementary School was in early December. I was assigned a seat in the middle of the class. I sat down and stared straight ahead at the teacher. I snuck peeks at the rest of the kids—all of whom were white. The boys wore fancy clothes like bell-bottom pants and shirts with Nehru collars. The girls had long clean hair and "flower-power" dresses on. I hadn't been in a classroom with just white kids before. I became extremely anxious and gradually lost my ability to concentrate. I was afraid to look up from my desk. I heard the teacher talking—but it seemed like she was in a different room. Seconds seemed like minutes and minutes seemed like hours.

As the day went on, I kept my head down and clenched the front edge of my desk with both hands. In my mind, the other kids were staring at me, talking about me, pointing at me, laughing at me, or thinking bad things about me. I couldn't find the courage to raise my hand to ask to use the bathroom. It was easier to just sit there and crap in my pants. As far as I could tell, no one noticed.

40

Within a week or two, Dennis and I were doing a lot of chores. After every meal, we washed, dried, and put away the dishes. We took turns on who would wash and who would dry. We used Brillo pads to scrub the pots. About once a week, we cleaned the inside of the refrigerator and oven, whether they needed it or not. Nellie Waterman was obsessed with having a clean oven, and we used Easy-Off every time.

We also dusted all the furniture in the living room, dining room, and master bedroom and then polished it with lemon Pledge. We vacuumed the carpets and cleaned the windows with Windex. We walked their dog. We made their bed. We were responsible for feeding and babysitting Anthony.

We took the garbage out and brought the cans in. We mowed and watered the lawn and handpicked any dandelions. We raked all the dead grass and leaves and disposed of both in the woods behind the house. For the first time in my life, I had blisters and calluses on my hands.

Nellie Waterman's sister Stella lived just around the corner—in a larger house with a bigger yard and a pool. She had an alcoholic husband, a teenage son, and two daughters that were in the same grades as Dennis and me. Dennis and I were at the beck and call of the daughters—and they knew it.

A 19-year-old girl named Midge also lived there—as a maid. Midge was from Chile and could barely speak English. Dennis and I helped her with dishwashing, laundry, vacuuming, dusting furniture, dog walking, and window cleaning. During the summer, we helped her with yard work and pool maintenance.

One day, I was trying to get some chlorine pellets to add to their pool. The pellets were in a large blue plastic container they kept alongside the back of their house. As I struggled to pry the lid off the container, the lid popped off and the container fell over. A plume of chlorine dust instantly got into my eyes, nose, and lungs. It felt like my lungs were on fire. I fell to the ground and struggled to breathe. Midge ran over to me and held my hand until I could stand up again. We both feared we would be in big trouble for what just happened. Midge panicked and began crying.

Dennis and I were used to Midge crying around *us*—she didn't do it in front of anyone else. Midge cried a lot—especially when we tried to talk with her about her life in Chile.

41

We got punished for many offenses: not cleaning well enough, not moving fast enough, asking the wrong question, asking for food, forgetting to do something, or doing something the wrong way, to name a few. Punishments consisted of being forced to stay in our room for many hours, being forced to strip down before getting beat with a belt, getting both open handed and backhanded smacks to our heads, and getting insults yelled directly into our faces.

One common punishment was administered in the Waterman's bedroom—while the Watermans lay in bed and watched television. Stripped down to just our white jockey briefs, Dennis and I had to face the wall near Isaac Waterman's side of the bed and hold our arms and legs spread out in the jumping-jack position. We were not allowed to move or lean against the wall. We held this position for hours and were only released to go to our beds when *The Tonight Show Starring Johnny Carson* ended.

This mode of punishment was exhausting, and if we turned our heads or let our arms fall, we were yelled at or walloped with a belt. The wall had just enough space for us to spread our arms out without touching one another. Hearing people laughing on the television shows made the punishment feel worse. I occasionally snuck a peek at Dennis to see if he was OK, and he did the same, to see if I was OK. I also did it to make sure that I wasn't alone. On one of those nights, the Watermans were watching the Apollo 11 moon landing. I was staring at a wall when I heard the scratchy voice of Neil Armstrong announce, *"That's one small step for man, one giant leap for mankind."*

The belt beatings were also done in the master bedroom, between the bed and the TV stand. Isaac Waterman grabbed one of our arms with his left hand and swung the belt with his right. We tried to escape the full brunt of the belt by running forward, but that just meant running in a circle—with Isaac Waterman at the center. His voice was full of rage. When he yelled, he squealed like Godzilla. The belt was usually directed at our asses and thighs. Sometimes, little pinhead-size drops of blood popped up right away where the edge of the belt landed. Bruises with shades of red, blue, and black showed up days later.

Nellie Waterman liked to yell insults directly into our faces.

"You're a useless son of a bitch!"

"You little bastard!"

"I oughta break your fucking neck!"

Her insults were occasionally backed up with slaps to our faces. She cocked her hand all the way back and walloped us. We got slapped with the front of her hand, with the back of her hand, when we least expected it, and when we fully expected it.

We did our best to placate Anthony at every turn, knowing to do otherwise might result in a "punishment." Anthony wanted everything—and he wanted it immediately. We were afraid to say no to him for fear of making him cry. Sometimes, Anthony cried no matter what we did. He even bit Dennis a few times. One of the bites broke through the skin on Dennis's back and left a deep, painful bruise. Dennis was afraid to tell anyone about the bite, but the pain eventually became too great for him to endure in silence. After he told Isaac Waterman what happened, Dennis was whisked off into the Watermans' bedroom, stripped down to his underwear, and beaten with a belt.

I stood outside the room, waiting for it to be over. Although he was a year younger than I was, the Watermans beat Dennis harder and more often than they beat me. Nellie Waterman once put a lit cigarette out on his forearm. I wondered how much he could take, and whether there was a breaking point—a point at which he might lose his grip on reality or die. Then, I'd be all alone. I imagined Dennis was good at borrowing sanity for the moment—for hell to pay later.

When the beating was over, Dennis came running out of the room with only his oversized white jockey underwear on. As he dashed into our bedroom, I saw red belt marks on the cheek of his ass and thighs—with urine streaming down his leg.

When we were being punished, we were not allowed to assume we were *not* being punished. We assumed we were in punishment mode until we were explicitly told we were not *currently* being punished. We had to ask to be sure.

"Am I still being punished?"

"Can I please be forgiven?"

"I'm sorry for what I did. Can I be forgiven now?"

If we were plainly told the punishment was over, we felt a great sense of relief. All that was left to do was hope another punishment didn't come too soon.

42

Despite their obsession with cleanliness in the living room and kitchen, the Watermans couldn't have cared less about the bathroom or our bedroom. We were not allowed to use the bathroom after our 7:30 p.m. bedtime. On nights when we had to pee, Dennis and I just urinated on the walls near our beds. We simply rolled our bodies toward the walls and "let it ride." The wall I urinated on was the wall which separated our room from the master bedroom. The smell in our room reminded me of the spots on subway platforms where men urinate against the walls. We eventually got used to it.

If necessary, we defecated in our closet. A loose piece of crudely cut linoleum covered the closet floor. The first time I did it was on Easter Sunday. We were being punished for something and were told to go in our room and close the door. We stayed there for hours, and I had an uncontrollable urge to defecate. I fought it off for as long as I could, hoping they would tell us our punishment was over—but that didn't happen. After I relieved myself on the closet floor, Dennis and I were terrified. We had no idea what they might possibly do to us for doing *that*.

They didn't even notice, so we did it whenever we were in the same predicament. It wasn't a big deal anymore. The stools eventually dried up, and we used a spatula to scrape them off the linoleum. The stains marking the

THE RIVER

perimeters of the stools weren't a big deal to us either—we just left them there. The bedrooms and bathroom smelled like a concoction of urine, feces, and baby powder.

43

We both had thick layers of dead, dirty skin on our scalps. I liked to scratch at the dirt and watch it come off in flakes. The flakes were tannish, about as thick as one or two playing cards and about the size of sesame seeds. Other parts of our bodies flaked as well—such as near our elbows and on the back of our necks. I knew other kids didn't have these flakes. My skin looked like paint chipping off the canvas of an old portrait. Our ankles and feet were especially dirty, with clearly visible filth caked on our skin. My underwear was a mess, and I tended to scratch my ass throughout the day.

One day at school, I was sitting in the classroom, scraping the flakes off my head and getting lost in a daydream. I started to push the flakes into a small pile in the center of my desk. When I snapped out of the daydream, I noticed a couple of my classmates were staring at me.

I somehow became comfortable working closely with a smart, spunky classmate named Virginia. She had long brown hair and wore fancy clothes. One day, I was working on an assignment with her and a couple of other kids at a table in our classroom. Virginia and I leaned slightly against one another, and I felt wonderful being so close to her. Then, without really thinking, I laid my head on her shoulder. I had become *too* comfortable.

THE RIVER

Virginia jumped up and screamed, "Gross! Get off me!" and ran out of the classroom as the other kids laughed aloud.

44

For breakfast, Dennis and I were each forced to eat one raw egg and one tablespoon of cod liver oil. It was gross—but it was all we got. We quickly slurped the eggs out of the bowls and then washed them down with the oil. The trick was to get it over with as soon as possible and not think about it while it was happening.

About once a month, the Watermans had us cook a large pot of sliced green peppers in olive oil. We then put five or six sliced peppers between two pieces of white bread and put the sandwich in a plastic bag. We did this over and over until the pot of peppers was done. Afterward, we brought all the sandwiches into the basement and put them in the freezer. We probably made fifty sandwiches at a time. Every morning, we went into the freezer in the basement and grabbed one pepper sandwich each for our school lunches. By lunchtime, the peppers were thawed, and the white bread was soaked with olive oil, making the sandwiches difficult to eat.

Dinner was the only substantive meal of the day for us. We were not allowed to speak during dinner—the frequently proclaimed Waterman motto was "Children are to be seen and not to be heard." They usually ate pasta for dinner but also stuff like pigs' feet, tongue, brain, liver, and tripe. We never ate any normal meat like steak or hamburgers or hot dogs. Dennis and I were mostly given liver and tripe, and I frequently had to fight off the urge to vomit. I had to disconnect my brain from my mouth, swallow the food, and be done with it. We were told we were not allowed to get up from the table until the food was done. On one occasion, we had tripe with linguine. Dennis hated tripe and spontaneously vomited some back onto his plate. They told him he could not leave the table until he finished it, vomit and all.

We were always hungry and thirsty. I snuck little bites of food from their refrigerator whenever I could, and many of my dreams involved searching for water. I also had asthma—and spent many nights struggling to breathe. What little sleep I got was often interrupted by nightmares involving me being kidnapped by a vicious witch. I was easy prey—as soon as I was aware of her presence, I became paralyzed. The witch would grab me when no one was looking and then lock me in a tiny closet that no one could ever find—or drag me deep into a lake where she tried to drown me. When I woke, I was afraid to move or breathe—or even open my eyes. I feared the witch was still under my bed, or sitting on the floor alongside my bed—with her angry face just inches from mine. I often went to school exhausted and riddled with anxiety.

Although both of us were filthy, emaciated, and bruised, it seemed like our teachers and social worker didn't notice. Our parents never made an issue of it either. Maybe they did—but to our knowledge, nothing was ever said or done to change anything. To be certain, the Watermans *never* took us to a doctor or dentist. The only time we did see a doctor was when we had a physical exam in school. The only thing I remember the doctor saying was "Cough."

45

On a visiting Sunday in the fall of 1968, my mother came to Little Flower accompanied by a man named John. He was around forty years old, stocky, and about five feet, ten inches tall. His brown hair was receding and combed back.

"Where's Dad?" I asked my mother.

Quietly, she explained, "I'm sorry, Kevin, but your father and I are no longer together."

I was shocked and confused. I started crying because I felt any hope of reuniting my family was lost. I also couldn't see how I would ever get out of the Watermans' house.

"John is a cook on a tugboat, honey," my mother told me.

"Is he your new husband?" I questioned.

"No, no, no! We're just friends, like boyfriend and girlfriend, you know? We met in Brooklyn, at a bar right down the street. We're just dating each other, honey. John was in the newspaper one time. He saved somebody's life in the East River."

Nodding, John agreed, "That's right, son. A guy fell off one of the piers, right into the river. I jumped into the river and helped him hold onto a ladder that was on the side of our boat. He was in big trouble. He definitely would've drowned if I hadn't done it."

THE RIVER

John seemed friendly enough to me, but I wondered why he was pursuing a relationship with my mother. She had so many kids ... and we were all in foster homes—and what about my father?

At the end of the visit, Dennis and I got into John's old blue station wagon, which was parked outside the Little Flower school. We were going to wait there until Mr. Dewey came to bring us back to the Watermans. Dennis was already in the second row, behind John, who was already in the driver's seat. My mother was sitting in the front passenger seat. I had just gotten into the seat behind my mother when I became aware of a car rapidly approaching us from our left side. I was startled enough to forget about closing my car door. The car stopped in front of John's station wagon, preventing us from leaving.

I looked at the driver and quickly realized that he was my father! He was crying and wore a tremendous look of anguish on his face. His passenger window was rolled down. It took me a second or two to see his right arm was stretched out and pointing a black gun straight at my mother. Both his forearm and hand were trembling.

"Watch out, Judy!" John yelled. "He's got a gun!"

"I'll kill you, you fucking whore!" my father screamed.

My mother didn't try to hide or duck—choosing instead to stare back at my father. "Go ahead, you fucking bastard! Shoot!"

"No, Judy—be quiet!" John pleaded.

She didn't listen, instead staring straight into my father's face and snarling, "Go ahead, you bastard! Pull the trigger! You ain't got the balls, do you? You fucking moron!"

Several seconds passed without any words spoken. My father's trembling hand kept the gun pointed at my mother. I was sitting behind her, looking directly at the gun. I thought about diving out of the open car door and onto the ground—but I was frozen. Seeing guns on television hadn't prepared me for being near a real gun—especially one held by my father and pointed in my direction.

The little black gun became the center of my universe. Although the whole experience lasted less than a minute, I spent months thinking about it. I couldn't stop replaying the experience over and over in my head. My father's hand shaking ... the look on his face ... the words that were said ... the open station wagon door ... the back of my mother's head ... and the black gun. Each rumination put me back at the same spot—wondering why my father's hand was shaking so much. If he was only trying to scare my mother, his hand wouldn't have shaken so much.

46

Miss Fogliano was my fifth-grade teacher. Most of what she said went in one ear and out the other. All I knew was that she was pretty and had short brunette hair and wore miniskirts. She also had a bad temper and liked to scream.

"I can't believe how dumb you all are!"

"Why do I constantly have to spoon-feed you?"

"Why can't you just do what you're told?"

Sometimes, she had to leave the classroom until she could act calm again. While the other kids feared her, I didn't. Compared to Nellie Waterman, she was an angel.

I talked while Miss Fogliano talked. I frequently got out of my chair without asking and cracked jokes at every opportunity. As a result, Miss Fogliano made me sit in class during recess and read stories from some boxes that were on the shelf by the windows. Each box was color coded and contained twenty laminated cards. Each card had a story about one topic or another, and I had to write a report on the story by the end of recess. The yellow box was easier to read than the red box, which was easier to read than the green box, which was easier to read than the black box.

I read about presidents, wars, inventors, foreign countries, African women with plates in their lips, Lapland, maps, and animals. The ocean was full of life! I learned some people also had horrible lives—but they still became famous! There were billions of people in all sorts of countries around the world, and most of them were happy. I saw my life was the exception—and not the rule.

I was usually the only kid getting punished in that manner, and I eventually completed all the cards. Nonetheless, I kept misbehaving. Miss Fogliano got so upset with me one day that she yelled at the rest of the class.

"I want everyone out of here now! Go to recess! Kevin— you stay."

She walked over to my desk, trying to remain calm as she asked, "What am I going to do with you, Kevin?"

"I don't know," I answered.

"Is it something *I'm* doing, Kevin? What's going on?"

"I don't know."

Several minutes of silence passed before she walked to the classroom door. Once there, she turned and, in a calm, deliberate voice, stated, "I want a four-page report from you telling me how you are going to improve your behavior. I want it by the time I get back from recess. That gives you thirty minutes. If it isn't completed when we get back, you're going to have to write an *eight-page* report during tomorrow's recess." Then, she turned around again and left the classroom.

I couldn't think of much to write about my behavior. Knowing recess only had twenty minutes left, and not the thirty minutes she claimed, didn't help at all—I didn't finish my report. I hardly slept that night, knowing I had to write eight pages within thirty minutes the next day.

Miss Fogliano seemed to enjoy telling the whole class about my predicament.

THE RIVER

"While we will be enjoying recess on this beautiful day outside, Mr. Weadock will have to write an eight-page report about how he can improve his behavior in class."

My classmates were more amused than upset to hear that.

"And single spaced, Kevin!" Miss Fogliano demanded as she walked out the door with the other kids.

I decided to start writing whatever came to my mind, almost random topics and thoughts. My fingers were still sore from the prior day's writing punishment, but they gripped hard to the tip of my pencil. The letters and words got bigger and bigger, and I didn't even care whether I spelled them correctly or stayed between the lines. I wrote long run-on sentences that drifted into and out of the events happening in my life at the Watermans' house. More and more erupted from my unconscious mind and found its way onto the paper. Eventually, I resorted to copying whatever I wrote on the first four pages—to the next four pages. I figured the things I was writing were so messed up that Miss Fogliano wouldn't be able to tell the difference. By the time Miss Fogliano and the other kids got back to the class, I had completed the assignment.

While everyone was getting in their seats, Miss Fogliano spoke.

"Well, class, let's see how your classmate Kevin did."

She focused her attention on me and demanded, "Kevin?"

"I'm finished," I announced.

"Oh really?" she asked with a surprised look on her face. "Then why don't you come up to the front of the room and read it to the class?"

I walked to the center of the front of the room and started reading what I wrote. I started off reading the words like someone else had written them, but the words became mine. I became angry, and started reading loudly.

"I'm a problem child and I am useless and I wish I drowned and I hate everyone more than they hate me even though they don't even know me or my brother Dennis. I got hit by a car twice but didn't die even though one of the cars was a Corvette and the tire on the other car hit my neck in the winter while I was riding my bike and my parents live in the city and they are alcoholics and I hate where I live now. I'm a foster kid and I want to go back to the city again because I have five other brothers and sisters you don't even know about. I'm dirty and stupid and people want to break my neck and I don't deserve to be near other normal kids. I should listen to Miss Fogliano but I don't care anyway because she only wants to get money and go home. I hate this school and I will punch anyone in the face if they even think about bothering me or Dennis and I mean it!"

Finally, Miss Fogliano shouted, "Stop reading, Kevin!"

I started crying in front of the whole class.

She quickly walked to where I was standing and gently grabbed my arm. She brought me to the nurse's office, where I lay down on a bench until the school day ended and it was time to get on the bus.

When I got off the bus, I was quickly surrounded by a group of boys.

"So, you're gonna punch us in the face, huh?" one of them asked.

"No!" I insisted.

"Kick his ass, Mark!" another boy crowed, egging on the tallest kid there.

THE RIVER

Sensing the inevitable, I punched Mark in the jaw as hard as I could. He was still holding his school bag when I hit him. My actions shocked him, and as the other boys waited for Mark to recover and retaliate, I ran away.

47

Almost a year after the incident with the gun, we were allowed to see our parents again at Little Flower. On our first visit back there, Mr. Dewey parked the car in the administration building's parking lot, turned the ignition off, and leaned back over his seat.

He informed us, "You're going to meet your new baby sister today, boys."

"What? I didn't even know my mom was pregnant!" I exclaimed.

"Oh?" he drawled. "She had the baby last year."

"How come we didn't know about it?" Dennis and I demanded in unison.

"I don't know. There must be *some* reason why they didn't tell you," muttered Mr. Dewey.

He picked up a piece of paper off the seat beside him. "OK, let's see ... ." He read for a bit and then announced, "Her name is Anne Theresa, and she was born ... she was born last July. Seems like she's been living with a foster family from Ireland. C'mon, let's go and try to find her."

The Irish people and Anne Theresa were at a picnic table near the pond, close to the administration building. The Irish lady had thick and wavy red hair and lots of freckles. She hugged me—and even called me "Love." The father was a lean man with receding hair and a happy-looking face. Anne Theresa was just over a year old and had started to walk. She had brunette hair and brown eyes, just like Mickey. While my family drifted off into various parts of the Little Flower campus, I stayed at the picnic table with the Irish people and Anne Theresa. The Irish man kicked and tossed a football with me for about an hour that day. He also spoke with me for a while, and he told jokes and kidded with me. Both he and his wife had strong Irish accents. They seemed to love my little sister, and I quickly decided I wanted them to adopt her so she could be spared the experience the rest of us had.

The car ride back from Little Flower, like all the other car rides back from Little Flower, was quiet. Mr. Dewey knew we were upset, and made simple attempts to get us to talk.

"So, how was it?" he asked.

"OK," we answered, in a dull and fading manner.

"Everyone alright? Did you see everyone?"

"Yeah."

Dennis and I didn't even talk to each other—we just looked out of our respective windows. We never knew why we were still in a foster home—or when our family would be back together again. I invariably wondered why one or both of my parents didn't just pack us all into a car and drive back to Jackson Heights or Rockaway Beach. That's what *I* would've done if *I* were them.

I had to find the right thoughts to be able to walk back into the Watermans' house again. I had to find a way to make the nightmare seem OK. I said hello to them when I entered their house, but inside my head was a cauldron of rage. I took it all out on Dennis. I called him mean names and bullied him whenever I needed to. I hated myself for this. I rationalized my behavior by telling myself Dennis needed to see and believe I was still strong and intact—that I hadn't caved in to the Waterman cruelty yet.

48

Nellie Waterman happened to be driving us on a road that passed through the town of Bohemia, the town where Paddy and Mickey lived. Sitting in the back seat, I looked around with the faint, naïve hope I might see my brothers somewhere. It was blind optimism, but by some miracle, I saw Mickey! He was walking on a sidewalk near a school and he was wearing a tan coat and thick black eyeglasses. They were the same coat and glasses he wore when we saw him on visiting Sundays.

"Stop!" I yelled.

"I see Mickey! Can we talk to him?"

"Absolutely not." snapped Nellie Waterman.

We had to stop at a traffic light, and Mickey kept getting closer to our car. Dennis and I waved our arms in the back window, trying to draw his attention. The light turned green and then Nellie Waterman sped away. I watched Mickey get farther and farther away until I didn't see him anymore.

Nellie Waterman called me into the kitchen that night. I could tell she was upset by the tone in her voice. I leaned my back against the oven, and she leaned over me, demanding, "Did you throw that fucking towel on the floor deliberately?"

"What towel?" I asked.

"The one laying on the floor in the bathroom, you fucking asshole!"

"No," I insisted. "I would never throw a towel on the floor!"

She struck me across my face with the back of her hand. The sharp blow got me trembling with rushes of fear and humiliation. She continued to yell directly into my face. While she was screaming, I thought that if I *really* wanted to, I could poison her—or set the house on fire with her in it.

49

It was still dark. I lay in bed and gently touched the side of my face where Nellie Waterman hit me. I wondered if I would wake up with a bruise on my face—or maybe even a black eye. I also thought about all the other stuff that had happened to me and Dennis in our two years at the Waterman's house. As I had done so many times before, I thought about running away. My thought process always stalled because I didn't know where to go, how I would get there, or if I would be caught and returned to the hands of the Watermans.

But this time felt different—I thought if I was quiet enough, I *could* sneak out of the house. I *could* escape. I *could* go somewhere else. If I didn't live at the Watermans' anymore, I *could* have a totally different life! The thought instantly purged all other thoughts from my mind. A bigger, braver version of me asserted himself inside my head and insisted on just one directive:

"Run away. Now!"

I sat up and slipped my feet into my slippers. I considered waking Dennis but sensed he might be too afraid to take such a risk. Worse, he might make enough noise to rouse the Watermans. I had to do this alone. I decided I'd try to get help for him after I got to wherever I was going. I slowly crept out of the room and toward the front door. As I approached the door, I realized I was only wearing my pajamas. I couldn't risk going back to the bedroom for my coat. I felt and heard the pounding of my heart. I was shaking—my mouth was dry.

I unlocked the front door, turned the handle, and pulled it toward me. I worried their dog might hear me and start barking. I slowly pushed the storm door open and stepped onto the stoop. I gently let the storm door close on the latch. I jumped off the stoop and onto the grass, running as fast as I could onto Waverly Avenue. My slippers somehow stayed on my feet. The air was so fresh and cold! As I ran at full speed into the night, I felt my heart and lungs working at their best—doing what I desperately needed them to do. I was experiencing pure freedom. No one was ever going to take this feeling away from me!

Two hundred yards of high grasses and weeds blanketed a field to my right. As I ran alongside it, I sensed a car with its headlights on—coming up behind me. I darted fifteen yards or so into the field, ducking down just enough to put myself at eye level with the top of the weeds. I watched the car drive past me and then stop at the traffic light at the corner of Waverly Avenue and Horse Block Road. I waited until the light turned green and the car drove away. I sprinted through the intersection and onto Horse Block Road. My instincts had taken over—I was heading back to Little Flower!

I kept running.

Horse Block Road led to the Long Island Expressway, which led to William Floyd Parkway, which led to the road that led to Little Flower.

I kept running.

Every time I sensed a car was coming, I hid in the woods or behind a building. Then, I ran again.

THE RIVER

Sunrise now allowed me to see if an approaching car was the Watermans' car. When I saw a car that was *not* their car, I put my thumb out like I was hitchhiking. A green van eventually pulled over on the *opposite* side of the street. The driver rolled down his window and yelled something to me that I couldn't understand. I ran across the street and told him I was going the *other* way, and not in the direction he was headed. He said he knew that—but would give me a ride anyway. I ran around the back of his van, opened the door, and climbed into the front seat. I was out of breath and frightened.

"So, where are you going?" the man asked. He seemed young—and had a walkie-talkie in his car.

"I'm going to the deli to get breakfast for my family," I declared.

He laughed and commented, "Wow, you're quite a kid! It's kind of unusual for a kid your age to be going out in his pajamas and slippers, so early in the morning, to get food for his family."

I said nothing. My mind was focused on whether the Watermans were coming after me. I stared through the rear window, expecting and dreading to see the Watermans' car in pursuit.

After a few minutes of watching my behavior, the man finally inquired, "Ok, little guy. What's *really* going on with you?"

I took a chance—and told the truth. I told him I was running away from a foster home that was being mean to me. I pulled up my pajama pants and showed him some fading welt marks left by a belt beating. I told him I had to leave my little brother there.

"I'm trying to get to Little Flower," I announced. "It's the place that put me in the foster home. I'm trying to see if they'll take us back. I know they will!"

The man responded, "Well, I think I might be able to help you. I'm a police officer."

My heart felt like it was going to jump out of my chest. I had no idea what was going to happen next. He could bring me back to the Watermans or to a police station. I might be in more trouble than I could imagine. I kept my right hand on the door's latch, just waiting for the opportunity to jump out—and run like hell.

Sensing I was starting to panic, he tried to calm me down, "Look, I promise I'm not going to bring you back to that home. I'll bring you back to Little Flower—just like you want. Let's see what *they* want to do, OK?"

He got on his walkie-talkie and informed someone that he had picked me up, that I was running away, and that he was bringing me to Little Flower in Wading River.

50

The policeman drove me directly to Father Fagan's house on the Little Flower campus. When we entered his house, Father Fagan was already dressed in his priest clothes: black pants and a black shirt with a priest's collar. He asked me to sit down on a couch in his living room and then went with the policeman into an adjacent room that looked like his office. While sitting on the couch, I leaned my body far enough to one side so I could peer through the open door of Father Fagan's office. The policeman was standing with his back to me, and Father Fagan was sitting on the edge of his desk with his arms folded. Their voices were so low I couldn't get a sense of whether Father Fagan was going to let me stay at Little Flower. After about ten minutes, the policeman walked out of the office, pointed his index finger at me, winked, and walked straight out the front door.

"Please come in here and sit down, Kevin," Father Fagan instructed.

I sat on the opposite side of his desk, the top of which was at my eye level.

He droned, "The policeman told me about what happened to you and your brother Dennis. Unfortunately, there is no room here for either of you right now. Until we can find a place for you and your brother, I think it's best that you remain at the Waterman home. I will personally speak to them and warn them not to hit you anymore."

"If I have to go back to the Watermans, I'll be back here tomorrow morning," I threatened.

After a long period of silence, I quickly switched to pleading, "Can't you just call those Irish people who have my little sister Anne? Maybe they'll take me in until you find another foster home for me and Dennis?"

Father Fagan stared at me for a while and eventually agreed, "OK, let's see what we can do here. Please go sit back on the couch."

After Father Fagan left the room, an old white lady dressed as a maid brought me a glass of milk and a slice of buttered toast. An hour later, Mr. Dewey showed up. He was reading from a piece of paper.

"OK . . ." he drawled.

"The names of the Irish people are Margaret and Tom Healy. I just spoke to them, and they've agreed to take you in until a bed opens up here at Little Flower."

"But what about Dennis?" I asked.

"Probably the same thing for him. For today, let's just get you out to the Healys."

51

I was still in my pajamas when I arrived at the Healys' house. It was a raised ranch on Grouse Drive in Brentwood, a town made up of miles and miles of streets laid out in a grid. The town was closer to New York City, a fact that somehow made me feel better about the tenuous situation I was now in. Margaret Healy was waiting on the driveway! She greeted me with a hug and her red hair got in my face and mouth.

I was surprised to learn that, in addition to my baby sister Anne, they had two of their own children. They both had blond hair and brown eyes—and politely said hello to me as I entered their house. Eileen was eleven years old, just like I was. Peter was ten years old, just like Dennis was.

Margaret Healy put her hand on my shoulder and walked me into a bedroom. As she pulled a few items out of Peter's closet, she asked, "So, how old are you, Love?"

"I just turned eleven about two weeks ago," I replied.

"Oh, then you're the same age as Eileen!" After her moment of excitement, she declared, "We'll have to get you out of those pajamas now."

"OK," I agreed.

I stripped—and felt a wave of embarrassment when I saw the grimace on her face.

She had seen the piss and shit stains on my underwear but didn't comment about them, instead inquiring, "How much do you weigh, Love?"

"The scale at my school said I'm almost sixty pounds," I told her.

"How did you get the bruises on your legs, Love?"

"They're from a belt," I admitted.

Before I knew it, Mr. Dewey was gone, I was in Peter's clothes, and Peter and I were playing stickball on the street in front of his house. To me, Peter seemed like a very nice kid—almost *too* nice. After he hit the ball to me, I threw it back to him so he could hit it again. While we were playing, two boys named Matt and Richard approached Peter and snatched away his bat. I didn't know exactly what was going on, but I stomped up to them to find out.

"Who are you?" they demanded.

"Kevin," I said.

To my surprise, Peter exclaimed, "Yeah, and he might be my foster brother soon so you guys better watch out!"

I sensed these kids had been messing with Peter quite a lot.

Indeed, Matt turned around and started to walk off with Peter's bat.

"Gimme my bat back, Matt!" yelled Peter.

In just a moment or two, I was in a fight! I punched Richard in the chest and grabbed the bat out of Matt's hands. I used the bat to chase them away, and we resumed our game of stickball. Peter laughed as he told his mother how I handled the situation.

Later that night, Margaret Healy told me that I needed to take a bath. I thought the Healy's were rich because of how clean their bathroom was. Margaret Healy knelt at the side of the tub and spoke to me with her Irish accent.

"Now don't be shy, Love. You'll need to take all your clothes off and hop into this hot bath I've prepared for you."

Until that point, I hadn't been nude in front of any female other than my mother. The water in the tub was so hot I had to go slowly into it. I confessed to Margaret Healy that I hadn't had a bath since I lived with my mother—and that the last time I took a shower was two years earlier at Little Flower.

Margaret Healy stayed in the bathroom with me. She gave me a washcloth and a bar of soap and guided me through the steps of cleaning myself. I was embarrassed at first, but soon realized I needed her help.

"Get all that stuff off your toes and feet, Love," she instructed.

After lathering up my head and scrubbing it with a washcloth, she used a small plastic bowl to rinse me.

"Any other bumps or bruises you want to tell me about, Love?" she asked.

"I don't think so," I said.

After getting all the dirty skin flakes off my scalp, she drained the tub and gave me a towel to cover myself. She scrubbed off the grimy film left in the tub and refilled it with hot water. As soon as she left the room I jumped back into the tub.

52

Margaret Healy was a hurricane of love and affection toward me. Tom Healy was kind, funny, and calm. They said that if I wanted to, I could call them Aunt Margaret and Uncle Tom. That was fine with me. I really didn't know how long I was going to be there and suspected I would probably be going back to Little Flower, anyway.

Tom Healy opened a fold-up bed for me in Peter's room, and Margaret Healy made the bed with clean sheets and a thick tan-colored wool blanket from Ireland. I wet the bed the first night I was there—and then tried to swap the sheets out for clean ones in the morning. Margaret Healy noticed my sneaky behavior and took the soiled sheets from me. She told me not to worry about them.

Since I wasn't enrolled in any school at the time, I stayed inside the house during the day and tried to stay busy while Peter and Eileen were at school. I played with their dog, made puzzles, and became familiar with all the Irish things they had in their house— shillelaghs of various configurations, small Irish and American flags coupled together in vases placed throughout the house, and the collection of Irish records they had.

On Halloween, Margaret Healy noticed me sitting on the floor—next to a cabinet below the kitchen sink. I was putting away all the pots and pans I had just cleaned. She became visibly upset, working herself into a state of mind somewhere between shock and rage.

"Why are you doing this, Kevin?" she asked sternly.

"I don't know," I replied. "I'm sorry."

"These pots are *already* clean!" she exclaimed.

"I'm sorry. I didn't know what else to do. This is what I always did at the Watermans'."

"Well, Kevin, cleaning pots and pans is *my* job," she scolded. "You should be playing outside, Love!"

When I stood up, she gave me a hug and kissed my hair and remarked, "You poor little man. Why don't you get on Peter's bike and ride around the neighborhood?"

Riding a bicycle again was a tremendous feeling. I hadn't been on a bike since I lived on 115th Street in Rockaway. Falling leaves swirled around me as I cut through one street and onto another. I didn't really know or care where I was going but loved my newly reclaimed freedom. I later dressed up like a hobo and went trick-or-treating—for the first time.

A few days after Halloween, I got on Peter's bike and explored the surrounding neighborhood. I rode up to their school, past the supermarket, and onto Wicks Road, a busy road that could take me to other towns. When I came back from my bike ride, Margaret Healy was waiting for me at the front door. She was smiling and waving her arms in a way that indicated she couldn't wait to get me in the house.

When I got inside, she gave me a huge hug and announced, "I have wonderful news, Love!"

She held me in her arms, even though mine remained hanging at my sides. As much as I needed to be loved, experiencing it felt strange. Margaret was open with her affection, but I wondered whether she might change her mind someday and not like me anymore.

"What? What is it?" I asked.

"Mr. Dewey called here when you were out. He said you can stay with us!" she exclaimed.

I asked her, "I don't have to go back to Little Flower?"

"No, you'll be staying with us now, Love!"

The news didn't feel real to me. How could such an incredible thing happen to *me*? There had to be a catch.

"What did Mr. Dewey say about Dennis?" I wondered.

Happily, she answered, "He said he'll pick up Dennis in a day or so to bring him here to live with us, too!"

I was reluctant to believe her and suspected Mr. Dewey might be lying. But it was true—Dennis *did* appear at the Healys' a few days later. As I feared, he had been roughed up by Isaac Waterman after I left. I could tell he was emotionally rattled as well—he wasn't acting right.

"They said that I knew you were gonna run away," he proclaimed.

"I told them I didn't know. I was just as surprised as them when I didn't see you in the morning."

The belt marks and bruises on his body looked different from the ones I was used to seeing. The bruises formed rings around his thighs, and a few spots were marred by deep cuts.

"He used the buckle side of the belt to hit me this time. See?"

Dennis pointed to a red-and-blue bruise that encompassed a gash shaped like a capital letter *L*.

53

A few weeks after Dennis moved in, Tom Healy added a set of bunk beds to Peter's small bedroom. As far as I knew, Peter was happy about the arrangement. Dennis and I certainly were, believing the addition of furniture meant we were going to live there for an extended period. We already loved the Healys and didn't want to be taken away from them. Our hopes were soon confirmed when Tom Healy asked us to sit with him at the kitchen table.

"I just wanted to let you know that we love having you both here, living with us," Tom Healy stated. "I hope you feel the same."

"Yeah, we do," I agreed, wondering what he was really trying to say.

Margaret Healy prompted, "Go ahead Tommy, ask them."

"I will, Maise—just hold on now," he replied.

Tom Healy continued, "Now that you'll be staying here, we want to know what you want to call us."

There was no doubt in my mind. He didn't need to say anything more.

"Can we call you Mom and Dad?" I requested quietly.

"Yes, but are you sure about this?" Tom Healy questioned.

"How about you, Dennis? Is that what you want, too?" Margaret Healy invited.

"Yes, that's OK. I guess I'm OK with that."

Tom agreed, "Well, that's OK with us, but it's important that you remember you really only have one *real* Mom and Dad, OK?"

****

Christmas came on quickly that year. The Healys were mad about Christmas! Christmas music played in the background for the entire day. Margaret Healy sang and hummed Christmas tunes while she cooked and worked around the house. I spent hours at the kitchen table with Eileen, making Christmas decorations out of paper, tape, crayons, glue, and glitter. Tom Healy drove us all into New York City to see *A Christmas Carol* at Radio City Music Hall. I was completely immersed in the movie and cried when Scrooge warmed up to Tiny Tim.

We attended a crowded midnight mass at St. Luke's church in Brentwood. I studied all the families that kneeled, then sat, then stood. Dennis and I were almost like them now. I was consumed by the joy around me and the smell of frankincense. I even took a chance at thinking that maybe there really was a God.

On Christmas morning, I got exactly what I hoped for—an electric football game that vibrated little football players up and down the field. I was also given the Beatles' *Abbey Road* album. Dennis and Peter each got a *Hot Wheels* set.

54

Tom and Margaret Healy were huge fans of President John F. Kennedy. They had a small collection of books and magazines about the Kennedy's, and a framed photograph of President Kennedy on the living room wall. They loved watching *The Lawrence Welk Show* on Saturday night, and they listened to albums from Irish comedians such as Hal Roach on Sunday afternoon. Sunday was also the day Margaret Healy prepared an Irish breakfast—a full "fry up" with blood pudding and all.

Tom Healy did all the plumbing, painting, carpentry, and electrical work that was ever needed in the house. He even installed a septic tank! He rented a jackhammer to bust up the front stoop and dug the hole with a shovel. He then hired someone to pull the old tank out and put a new one in. He loved green, so *everything* was green. The outside of the house and the carpets in the house were green. The furniture was upholstered in green fabric. When the time came to replace the driveway, he added a green pigment to the concrete. He built a green playhouse in the backyard that was big enough for Eileen and a friend or two to play inside. It even had a kitchen with a fake oven and sink.

I came to learn that his mother had died giving birth to his younger brother Patrick. His father also died when he was a young boy. Along with his siblings Maureen and

Patrick, he was raised by his Aunt Nancy in Elphin, a small village in County Roscommon. Margaret Healy was also born into poverty, and her family worked as servants and laborers in Cong, County Mayo. They both immigrated to the United States in the early 1950s, and Tom Healy soon joined the U.S. Army. A mutual friend introduced them to each other while they were leaving a church in Brooklyn.

Margaret Healy took care of all the health care requirements for Dennis and me. I had frequent asthma attacks—two of which were so severe I had to be hospitalized at Smithtown General hospital. Each hospitalization required doctors to put me in a humidified oxygen tent for a week. Neither my mother nor father visited me while I was in the hospital.

I had to use an inhaler and take several medicines—three times per day. I also had to get allergy shots once a week. Margaret Healy made sure I took my medicine—and if I wasn't home when the next dose was required, she walked around the neighborhood to track me down. I had thirty-four cavities on my very first visit to a dentist! It took many dentist appointments to get them filled. Since Margaret Healy didn't drive, we used taxis to get to and from the appointments.

I began to learn what living in a stable home was like. We had a little black dog named Smokey. I had a paper route. I played baseball for the St. Luke's CYO team. Dennis joined the Cub Scouts and proudly wore his Webelos uniform around the neighborhood. Our creepy life at the Watermans' was behind us. Dennis and I were treated as true members of the family when we visited the Healys' relatives. We gained an Uncle Jack and an Aunt Maureen, an Uncle Frank and an Aunt Theresa, and many cousins as well. Their relatives gave us Christmas gifts and even mailed us birthday cards with money inside!

Although a chain smoker, Tom Healy didn't drink alcohol. He rarely used foul language, and tried his best to be fair and friendly to everyone he met. He worked twelve-hour days, six days per week, at Ogden Foods in Queens. He spent Sunday evenings at the kitchen table—working on "the figures," which were long handwritten spreadsheets reflecting inventory and revenue from the vending machines he managed.

Margaret Healy made the same dinner for him every night: potato pancakes, ham steak, turnips, and hot tea. Dessert was coconut custard pie. While he ate, one or more of us sat around the kitchen table to talk with him. I wondered why he was giving us advice all the time. I didn't feel like I needed it—and thought he was just an old person talking to me about old people stuff.

"If you ever find yourself in a jam, you can always call me or Mom. We won't ask any questions. Will we, Maise?"

"No, Tommy, we won't," she agreed.

"Did you hear Mom, Kevin?"

"Uh huh," I grunted.

"And life is always worth living, no matter how dark things seem. There is always light at the end of the tunnel, Kevin."

"Uh huh."

"You've got your whole life ahead of you now, so let's forget about the past."

"That's right, Tommy," Margaret Healy declared. "What's done is done."

"Do you understand, Kevin?"

"Uh huh."

55

The air was cool and crisp—fall had arrived. Dennis and I were visiting my mother and John in their basement apartment near the corner of 3rd Avenue and 47th Street in Brooklyn. They had a large German shepherd named Heidi. John took a lot of pride in Heidi, and talked about her as she sat by his feet.

"She comes from a champion line of German shepherds," he boasted. "And we've got the paperwork to prove it. Right, Judy?"

"Yes, somewhere around here," my mother agreed.

I noticed my mother was pregnant, but I was afraid to ask her about it. Dennis was less restrained.

"Are you pregnant, Mom?" asked Dennis.

"Yes, honey," she answered. "I'm going to have a baby in a couple of months."

We visited them again just before Christmas. My mother had given birth to a baby boy named Freddie. He seemed too skinny and weak to me.

"Is he OK, Mom?" I asked.

"Yes, honey. He'll be OK."

I argued, "But he looks so weak, Mom!"

"Freddie has Down syndrome, honey."

I knew what *that* was, and said nothing more.

On one of the nights we were there, Paddy and Katie stopped in. They had been visiting my father in

Jackson Heights and took the subway to see us in Brooklyn. They were fifteen and sixteen now, respectively—teenagers on the other side of puberty. Paddy had grown his hair long and was almost six feet tall. His lip and chin sported a coating of peach fuzz. Katie was about six inches taller than me. She also had long hair—and breasts! I was afraid Paddy and Katie were no longer interested in being my big brother and sister. They wore hippie clothing and seemed to talk in a language that separated us. While Katie was still bubbly and affectionate, there was a distance between Paddy and me that made me nervous.

Since Paddy and Katie were now there, my mother and John felt free to go out to a nearby bar. While they were gone, Paddy and Katie hung out in the bedroom and drank beer. Dennis and I sat on the couch near Freddie's crib in the living room and watched television. Paddy and Katie later joined us in the living room. Now drunk, they talked about things that happened when we lived as an intact family in Rockaway Beach. One of their stories involved a situation where my parents were drunk and arguing in the living room of our apartment on 115th Street. They remembered that my father punched my mother in her stomach. She fell over in pain and spontaneously aborted a fetus in the living room. Katie said she saw my father carry the fetus to the bathroom and flush it down the toilet. I imagined the fetus was the same size as a newborn puppy—and that it still had the slimy membrane around it. I wondered if it was still alive when it got flushed—and if the story was even true.

My mother and John eventually came back to the apartment—drunk. As soon as they fell asleep, Dennis and I decided to join Katie and Paddy on their way back to Jackson Heights. We boarded the RR train and settled in for the long ride through Brooklyn, Manhattan, and Queens. Besides us, there were just a few homeless people sleeping on the other end of the subway car. Paddy was so drunk that he laid down on the seat and passed out. He vomited on the floor a few times, and when the train stopped or started, his vomit trickled along accordingly. A policeman came into our car and banged his baton hard against the seat, about six inches away from Paddy's head. Even with that, Paddy could barely wake up.

We never did find our father that night. We wound up back in Brooklyn instead—just as the sun was rising. Dennis and I went back to the Healy's the next day. Some months later, Freddie was struck with pneumonia and passed away.

56

My father sometimes drove his white 1965 Mustang out of the city to visit us in Brentwood. I'd stare out the living room window and wait for his car to pull up on the driveway. On one of those visits, another man got out of the car with my father. As they entered the house, I noticed the other man was the same height and weight as my father ... and they both had black hair and brown eyes ... and the same space between their top two front teeth.

My father cut the suspense, proudly revealing, "This is my son Dan."

"I didn't know you had another son, Dad!" I exclaimed.

"He looks exactly like you!" Dennis pointed out.

My father explained that he had been married in Ireland before coming to America—and Dan was his son from that marriage. Dan said he was an accountant and lived in Manhattan. He seemed disturbed to see us, especially in the setting of a foster home.

"I've got—" he stammered, "I mean you've both got—I mean all three of us have twin sisters in Ireland too!"

After taking a moment to collect himself, Dan continued, "They're technically your half-sisters, but they're your sisters, nonetheless. Their names are Elizabeth and Margaret."

In shock, I grunted, "Uh huh."

I kept staring at Dan that day, trying to figure out what he thought of us, and whether we were now going to see him more often—or if this was the only time we would ever see him. The shocking news of a half-brother and two half-sisters, a prior marriage and family, and the uncanny resemblance between Dan and my father had unsettled me. Even the Healys didn't know how to process the new information.

Margaret Healy quickly boiled up some tea for everyone and put a coffee cake out on the dining room table.

"I'm not in the mood for tea, Margaret," my father declared. "But I sure could use a stiff drink, if you've got any of that."

Other than a single highball they sipped on New Year's Eve, the Healys didn't drink alcohol. They kept just a few bottles of whiskey and vodka in a dining room cabinet—for friends and relatives who occasionally stopped by.

With a reluctant smile on his face, Tom Healy put a bottle of whiskey and two shot glasses on the table. My father and Dan each downed a few shots of Dewar's whisky while the rest of us ate cake and drank tea.

57

Dennis and I visited my father in the city on several occasions. We spent our time with him bouncing from one Irish bar to another. It was the same ritual in each of these bars—my father drank with his friends at the bar while we drank soda and played 8-Ball. His friends liked to talk to us and buy us potato chips and soda. My father made sure we knew which county in Ireland they came from.

Mickey met us in the city during one of our visits. On this day, my father was eager to introduce all three of us to his friend John Cudahy, who was an accountant with a small office on 73rd street, just off Roosevelt Boulevard in Jackson Heights. As we walked to his office, my father told us that if Mr. Cudahy asked us where we lived, we should each say we live in Jackson Heights—with my father.

Mr. Cudahy was bald and stout and well into his sixties. He reminded me of the wizard in "*The Wizard of Oz.*" He guided us to a small room at the back of his office. There were a few folding chairs in front of his desk for us to sit on. Dozens of boxes of paper were loosely stacked up against the wall behind his desk. After fielding a few questions from Mr. Cudahy, who was sitting down in his chair and leaning forward to speak with us, I realized my father wanted to claim all three of us as dependents on his tax return. I thought this would be a good thing for my father, so I became adamant about living on 74th Street. I guess our collective bullshit stories didn't make sense though, because Mr. Cudahy grimaced as he looked at my father, who was standing behind me.

"I'm sorry Pat, I can't do it. It won't go through," he said.

"Well, it never hurts to try!" my father laughed.

Later that day, my father took all three of us to the construction site where he was working—the World Trade Towers in Lower Manhattan. We were excited because the buildings were going to be the tallest in the world, even taller than the Empire State Building.

When we arrived at the site, we saw many types of trucks and tractors moving around. The jackhammers and generators were so loud that we couldn't hear each other. We passed through a few gates and a few doors and eventually boarded a huge freight elevator. Within seconds, we were zooming upward—on our way to the seventy-seventh floor.

"Now, all of the Irishmen you're going to meet up here are in the Local 608 Carpenters Union," my father explained. "They're working overtime, so they'll be bringing home a pretty penny."

My father and the guys he introduced to us laughed a lot and spoke in Irish brogues. They drank shots of whiskey from a bottle in a paper bag.

One of the men who wasn't drinking showed us how a helium-neon laser level worked. The device was about the size of a vacuum cleaner canister, and he aimed it across the entire seventy-seventh floor.

"Go to the other end of the building to see a fuzzy little red dot on the wall," the man instructed. It seemed like a magic trick to me!

The man then walked over to a stack of blueprints that were loosely spread out on top of a pallet of sheetrock.

"These big sheets of paper tell us where all the walls and electrical outlets need to be placed," he said.

We saw how they used blue chalk lines to mark the locations of interior walls. To my surprise, the studs they were setting up for the sheetrock were made of aluminum. All around us, drills buzzed loudly as the workers drove in the screws. The floor didn't have any windows yet, just rectangular openings that led to the cold air outside, seventy-seven floors above the street.

"You're in the South Tower now, boys," the man declared. "Look out one of those windows and take a gander at the North Tower. These buildings are swaying with the wind!"

"You bet your life they are," my father laughed.

I couldn't detect any swaying in our building. Just like the man said, I had to watch the *other* tower. The swaying was indeed noticeable, especially at the higher floors such as the seventy-seventh. I thought it was amazing that "the world" allowed buildings to sway.

"Why doesn't the building crack?" I wondered aloud.

"Talk to the engineer, son," my father instructed, pointing to the man who had shown us the laser and blueprints. "They've figured it all out. They built this whole fucking city, son. This city will scare the bejesus out of you!"

"Think about how a tree stands up to hurricanes," the engineer told us.

My father contributed, "Listen to him, lads. This is engineering!"

"If the building *couldn't* sway, it might crack when strong winds hit it," the engineer explained.

My mind started running with the understanding that the things humans made were just imitations of what nature taught us. The biggest and strongest things in the world still had to bend to survive. I suddenly considered engineering the highest form of thinking, above sports and music and medical stuff. *Everything* seemed to depend on engineering.

I stood as close to the open windows as I could without being afraid, marveling at "engineering." Then, my fear of heights took over. I felt that if I went too close to the window, an invisible force beyond my control might suck me out of the building. I backed away.

Mickey was different: with his hands anchored inside, he leaned forward until his head was completely outside. He looked at the street below and then out over Brooklyn towards Coney Island. He then rotated his head and shoulders so he could look up to the top of the South tower. He clearly had no fear of heights. The realization saddened me. My brother was growing up somewhere else, far away from me.

THE RIVER

58

I only saw Donna and Timmy when we visited my mother, which was once or twice a year. When I did see them, we merely said hello to each other, and then they scurried away to play or watch television together. They seemed like happy kids, always smiling and looking for fun. Timmy had dark brown hair and was skinny like the rest of us. Donna's hair was still as blonde as it ever was.

I never really knew when I might see Katie, Paddy, or Mickey. Our occasional meetings seemed to happen with little notice or planning involved. Katie showed up unannounced at the Healy's one summer day. She was seventeen years old and had hitchhiked over forty miles from her foster home in Southampton. She was with another girl her age, and they both looked like hippies—wearing maxi dresses and hair down to their waists.

I was so happy to see her! I told her all about my new life at the Healy's home. I naively hoped another miracle might happen that day—that she too could live with me and Dennis at the Healy's—but she was gone in a few hours. Tom Healy drove her and her friend back to Southampton.

I learned that Paddy, who was now sixteen, was living with my father in Jackson Heights and now wanted to be called Pat. Sometime near Christmas, Dennis and I visited him at my father's apartment on 74th Street. The entrance to the apartment was at the back of the house. A tight spiral of wooden stairs led to the third floor. When we walked into the living room, Pat was slouched on the couch, smoking a cigarette, and listening to "*A Day in the Life*" from the *Sargent Pepper's Lonely Hearts Club Band* album. The music was coming from a small record player he had placed on the floor. I immediately noticed hundreds of brown spots on the ceiling and walls.

"Hey, Pat, what are all these slimy brown spots? It looks like spit or snot!"

"You're right—they're my spit marks."

"What?" I gaped. "Why?"

"I like to spit. I drink Coke while I'm eating black licorice—and then I spit wherever I want to. You need to let it sit in your mouth first so the spit gets all thick and brown. Then it's sticky enough to stay on the ceiling. I like watching it drip from the ceiling."

The stuff Pat was saying just didn't make sense to us, and we started to laugh. We stopped when we realized Pat didn't think it was funny. He jumped off the couch and started yelling at us.

"I hate living here! I wish I was back with Mickey at the Kowalskis'... but now I'm stuck here! I don't know anyone in this neighborhood—and Dad's always at the fucking bar!"

His anger boiled over into every word. The only thing that seemed to placate him was his guitar. When he played it, his long hair fell forward to cover his face, and he tuned out the rest of the world.

"So where is Mickey, anyway?" I asked.

Pat explained, "Dad made some arrangement with Little Flower. He picked me up one night at the Kowalskis'. We didn't even know he was coming! He told the

Kowalskis, 'I want my son Patrick, right now!' and that was it."

"And what about Mickey?" I asked.

"We left him there. It was hard. He watched us drive away. He cried on the driveway when we got in the car. He was screaming for Dad to take him, too, but Dad just drove away."

"Oh my god!" I cried. "I feel so bad for Mickey!"

"Why didn't Dad take him back, too?" asked Dennis.

Pat sighed, "I don't know why, Dennis. I don't know what to do. I feel like it's my fault."

59

Our new social worker was a young and pretty lady named Miss Bartolo. She arranged for all my brothers and sisters, including Donna and Timmy, to meet at a park where the Long Island Sound rushed in to fill a pond near the shore. The pond was inhabited by many young bluefish called "snappers." I was excited to see my brothers and sisters again. We spent much of the visit running around the perimeter of the shallow pond and trying to catch fish with our hands. Miss Bartolo spent time with each of us separately and eventually came over to talk with me.

"Will our family ever get back together again?" I asked.

"I think so, Kevin. But since your mom and dad are no longer together . . ."

"I know," I said. "We have to pick one, right?"

"That might be what happens, Kevin. Do you ever think about it?"

"Nah, not really," I told her.

Several months later, my entire family was in the lobby of the Queens Family Court House in Jamaica, Queens. It wasn't our first visit. I hated court dates. My poor and broken family was on display for the rest of the world to see. The shame engulfed me.

Miss Bartolo walked us—one at a time—into a courtroom while the rest of us stayed in the lobby. I had my turn too. A few policemen stood in the corners of the courtroom while other people sat at desks. A judge sat behind a high counter. Miss Bartolo and I walked up to the counter. I had to take a couple of steps backwards so I could see him.

"Hello, Kevin," he said with a smile.

"Do you know why you are here today?"

"No," I replied.

"I'm interested in how you feel about your parents, Kevin."

"OK."

"I imagine you love them both, Kevin. Am I right?"

"Yes."

"I thought so, Kevin. I know that talking about your parents isn't easy—especially in this big room … but I just want to know if you have ever felt afraid around either of them. Can you tell me?"

I thought of telling him about how scary it was for me to be near my father when he was angry—especially when we talked about my mother. My father's face and voice changed in a twisted and sardonic way as he told us our mother was a "filthy fucking whore." He followed it up with the usual "and she has gone ahead and destroyed us all now." He laughed in a contemptuous way when reminding us she had been committed to Bellevue and Creedmoor psychiatric hospitals "on multiple occasions." I wasn't ready or able to explain all of this to the judge in the open air of the courtroom. I luckily remembered another moment that I felt I *could* talk about.

"Well, I felt afraid around my father one time," I volunteered.

"Please tell me about that time, Kevin."

"Well, we were in Captree Bay, fishing for fluke, and the boat we rented had drifted into some shallow water in the middle of the bay. The water was calm and clear, and we could easily see the sand under the boat. My father asked us if we wanted to jump out and swim around. We were a little scared, but we did it anyway. It was only about three feet deep."

"Please continue, Kevin."

Glancing around the courtroom, I went on, "Well, my father and the boat started drifting far away from us."

"Continue, Kevin."

"I was afraid my father would leave us there," I admitted, looking at the floor beneath my feet.

"Thank you, Kevin. Please be seated."

A few months later, Margaret and Tom Healy sat down with us at the kitchen table to let us know we were going to live with my mother. I didn't know it at the time, but my mother and John were renting a house up in the Catskill Mountains, about a hundred miles north of New York City. Although we loved the Healys, the chance to live with our brothers and sisters again was a dream come true.

When Margaret Healy told me the exact date we were leaving, I started to calculate how many days and hours and minutes remained. I wrote the numbers on a sky-blue plastic tissue dispenser that was on a nightstand near my bed.

Margaret Healy walked into my room one morning and noticed me writing the numbers on the tissue dispenser.

She asked, "What are these numbers, Kevin?"

I could see she was upset.

"Are we so bad that you're now counting the hours and minutes to get away from us?"

THE RIVER

"No, no, no, Mom!" I cried. "I haven't been with my family in so long! I miss them! I'm sorry, Mom!"

We left the day after the school year ended. Margaret Healy started sobbing as soon as Miss Bartolo's blue van pulled into our driveway. I felt like I was betraying her by getting into the van.

60

After a couple of hours on the New York State Thruway, we pulled up in front of an old country home that sat on the highest point of Cauterskill Road in Catskill, New York. Mickey was there on the gravel driveway when we arrived. He couldn't wait for us to open the car doors, so *he* did.

"Hi, Dennis! Hi, Kevin!" he yelled, even more excited than I was. "Man, you're not gonna believe how many ponds and streams there are around here. They're all on our property, too!"

My mother and Katie came out of the house with Donna and Timmy tagging along behind them. Donna, now almost 10 years old, called our names and ran with open arms to the car. Timmy was eight and approached us far more tentatively. The experience was surreal for me. I had only dreamed we would all be living together again. After a few minutes of hugs and pure joy, we walked inside the house.

The home was rustic, maybe a hundred years old, but its interior was nice, which surprised me. It had wide wooden plank flooring, high ceilings, a spacious kitchen, a living room, and a large front porch. There were several bedrooms upstairs. There was even a tiny bungalow with a porch in the backyard.

Three German shepherds also lived in the house; Heidi had given birth to puppies, and my mother had decided to keep two of them. They were about nine months old. The female dog had a silver coat, and the male dog, Dylan, was black and brown.

My mother offered, "The silver dog can be your dog, if you want it, Kevy."

"Really? This can be *my* dog?"

"Yes, Kevy. Yes!"

"OK, then I want her. I want her! She's *my* dog!"

Feelings of joy started compounding inside me, and I became hysterical. The dog was beautiful, and I loved her at once. I named her Bonnie, right there and then, after the little girl I "married" when I lived on 96th Street.

"Your brother Pat is out back in the bungalow," my mother said.

Excited to see him, I ran to the bungalow. Pat was sitting on an old couch that was on the porch. I could hear Neil Young's *"Southern Man"* coming from the inside of the bungalow.

"Hey, Pat!" I yelled.

"Hey," he said in a low voice, not even flashing a smile.

He remained seated, leaning back on the couch, and smoking a cigarette. He didn't look at me or stand up to say hello. He just stared straight ahead.

I stopped walking toward him and murmured, "OK, see ya." I turned around and trudged away, hurt by his lack of interest in me. I didn't know what to think.

"Pat's all fucked up, Kevin," Katie told me. "He's been drinking and smoking pot all day. Talk to him tomorrow."

Mickey was standing in the kitchen, waiting for me to come back into the house. At fifteen, he was well into puberty and had grown to be more solid than I was, with a stocky frame and thick thighs. I was still a skinny little kid. We spent a good part of that day running around the property and wound up at a house that was at the base of the hill, near Kaaterskill Creek. Two other kids our age were shooting an old .22-caliber rifle at tall wooden poles that held high-voltage lines. The poles were about a hundred yards away from us. We took turns shooting the gun. My first couple of shots missed. I wanted to try another time, so I quickly reloaded. As I started to raise the rifle, another kid tried to snatch the gun away from me. My finger was on the trigger, and his tug caused the gun to fire. The bullet went through a portion of his T-shirt near his ribs.

Rattled by what almost happened, I started walking back up the hill toward the house. Mickey soon ran up alongside me.

"What the fuck is wrong with that gun, Mickey? I could have killed that kid!" I yelled.

"I know," he announced. "That's the same gun Pat shot Timmy with."

"What? Pat shot Timmy?" I asked in disbelief.

"Yeah, in the neck."

We stopped walking.

"Are you kidding me, Mickey?" I demanded, hoping he'd say yes.

He responded, "Kevin, look at Timmy's neck when you get home."

As soon as I walked into our house, I walked up to Timmy and checked his neck, to see whether Mickey was telling the truth. Timmy had a small pink scar on one side of his neck and a longer pink scar on the other side.

61

The boys at the bottom of the hill shared their fireworks with Mickey and me on the Fourth of July. I eventually got bored with the whole thing and walked back up the hill to our house. When I arrived, I discovered that, except for Donna and Timmy, everyone was drunk. All they could do was lie around on the couch or beds, seemingly unconscious. Even Dennis, who was just under thirteen years old, had vomited in multiple locations. I noticed a couple of empty gallon bottles of pink Chablis in the garbage. There were also a few unopened half-gallons stored for later. I promptly poured them into the sink.

    I walked down the hill again, hoping to play with the other boys and their fireworks. Halfway down the hill, I saw Mickey standing by himself near a swing set. As I walked toward him, I noticed an adjacent pond full of turtles sunbathing on logs. Fish swam just below the surface, and butterflies and other sorts of little flying bugs zoomed just above. Lilies cradled large frogs and served as springboards for their occasional jumps into the calm water. I knew Mickey and I were going to love that pond, and thoughts of all the fun we could have helped me forget about the drunk people back at the house.

    I saw Mickey had already caught some frogs from the pond. The remains of dozens of frogs dripped from the links of the chains that held the swings up. Other frog parts littered the ground below. Bits of frog bodies had dried between some links, and frog heads dangled from others.

Mickey paid little attention to me. He focused instead on walking near the pond's edge to find more frogs to blow up. He cried and stammered as he talked about everyone being drunk. After catching a frog, he walked back to the swing set and pushed its head through a link in one of the chains, not caring how much pressure he put on the frog's head or arms. Once its front half was inside the link, the frog was stuck there. Mickey jammed a firecracker between the frog's body and the link and used a match to light the fuse.

62

The vomit on the kitchen and living room floors told me everyone was drinking pink Chablis again. Disgusted, I walked out of the house and down the hill, toward the town of Catskill.

Mickey saw me as I was walking away and asked, "Where are you going, Kevin?"

"I'm leaving. I want to live with Dad. These people are fucked up."

"Well, then I'm coming, too," he yelled, quickly catching up.

As we walked, my dog Bonnie ran after us. She followed for about a mile. Although almost full grown, she was still a puppy. Her tail was wagging and one of her ears was flopped over. She wanted to stay with me! Leaving Catskill meant I had to leave her behind. I was tempted to turn around—just so I could still have her in my life. A horrible feeling settled in my stomach. I wanted her to go back to the house—but I didn't know how to make her. I started hitting her and yelling at her until she finally walked away. I hated myself more than ever.

Mickey and I hitchhiked ten miles to the train station in Hudson, New York. We jumped the first southbound Amtrak train and took a seat. Neither of us had any money, so when we heard the conductor nearby, we hid in the restroom. Someone must have told the conductor we were hiding in there because he banged on the door and demanded that we get off the train at the next stop. We got off in a town called Rhinebeck and went into a quiet little bar near the train station. We begged the bartender to give us each a glass of soda and a bag of potato chips. As we sat there eating the potato chips, we overheard him telling someone that he was thinking of calling the police on us. We decided to leave the bar and hang out by the train station instead. We "boarded" the next Amtrak train and hid in the bathroom again. We arrived at Penn Station just before midnight.

For the next few weeks, Mickey and I hung out with my father, who was collecting unemployment at the time. We passed the time in Irish bars surrounding the Roosevelt Avenue subway station. We drank soda, played pool, watched Yankee games on television, and ran bets for all the guys at the bar to the Off-Track Betting building on Roosevelt Avenue. Mickey and I also spent many days walking around the neighborhood, occasionally taking turns kicking a stone as far as we could.

Our father felt bad about our daytime idleness, so he arranged for us to stay the last two weeks of the summer at Aunt Sis's rooming house in Rockaway Beach. We spent our days fishing off the Cross Bay Bridge, roaming around Rockaways' Playland, and watching television in Connolly's bar. We were transfixed by the Munich Olympics and the horrific drama that unfolded there.

63

That fall, I enrolled in ninth grade at Newtown High School in Elmhurst, Queens. Mickey and I took the subway from Jackson Heights to Elmhurst and back each day. We attended classes for about three weeks or so before deciding that the shopping mall on Queens Boulevard was more fun. We also walked the streets of Jackson Heights on many days, getting by with just the few dollars my father gave us each morning. He had no idea we weren't going to school. We met up with him in the evening at one of the Irish bars he went to after work.

My father stood when he drank—belly to the bar, occasionally twisting his torso to the left or right to yuck it up with the bartender or another man. He kept his drinking money on the bar—loosely arranged bills from breaking a twenty or fifty-dollar bill. I even saw a hundred-dollar bill get changed once. Within a foot of his money was a shot of whiskey, a glass of beer, and a soft pack of Camel cigarettes.

While Mickey and I played 8-Ball, we snuck peeks at my father's drinking money. He easily spent twenty to thirty dollars a night on drinks. The tips he gave the bartender far exceeded the few dollars Mickey and I split each day. And then there were his sports bets placed with the bookie at the back end of the bar. Some of my father's money passed through my hands too—when I ran his track bets up to the OTB on Roosevelt Avenue. Among his usual bets was the 3-1-7 Trifecta, the numbers signifying his birthdate, St. Patrick's Day. He occasionally won hundreds of dollars, and even won a Super Bowl pool for five-thousand dollars.

My father's callous attitude towards us, especially regarding money, enraged Mickey. He stomped around the apartment and mumbled under his breath. I even noticed tears in his eyes a couple of times. He wanted to spend more time by himself now, and I wasn't sure of what he did or where he went during the day. I took to walking around the neighborhood on my own. I came home one day to find Mickey standing in the center of our living room with a funny look on his face.

"What's going on Mickey?" I asked.

He smiled and pulled ninety dollars in small bills from his front pants pocket. "Here," he offered, "You take forty."

I smiled and accepted the wad of cash. "Where did you get it?" I wondered.

He pointed to a door which separated our apartment from a stairway that went into the landlord's apartment downstairs. The door was locked from the landlord's side.

Mickey explained, "I know how to open the door without them knowing."

He got caught red-handed on his next attempt—the landlord was waiting in hiding for him.

64

Mickey's temper began to flare more frequently, and he had a hard time reining himself back in when it did. My father threw gasoline on the fire by taunting Mickey when he was upset—calling him names like "Sasquatch" and "The Little Giant" in front of the other barflies. Mickey hated these names—both meant to mock his height. While Katie, Pat, Dennis, and I were growing up to be long and lean, Mickey was three to four inches shorter and had a stockier frame. What he lacked in height he made up for in rage. My father's teasing left Mickey humiliated, mumbling under his breath, and very often so upset he couldn't speak without trembling. I kept my mouth shut, hoping he could settle down and we could go about the business of being brothers again.

Still, Mickey and I did argue at times, usually over chess games or other trivial subjects such as who was the best player on the Yankees. One of our arguments led to a fight in our apartment on an unseasonably hot afternoon in October. Mickey took a wild punch at my head and missed, striking the door behind me instead. After hearing how hard his fist hit the door, I ran away from him and into the front room of the apartment, which was our father's bedroom. We started wrestling on our father's bed, then rolled around the floor trading headlocks, elbows, and punches to the ribs and face. Although we were both out of breath and sweating profusely, the fight kept going. I was frightened because Mickey was stronger than me, and I didn't know how our brawl might end. Anything seemed possible. I was willing to stop—but Mickey wasn't. I was left with the option of either escaping from the apartment or trying to knock him out.

We continued to punch each other and wrestle, and we were again fighting on our father's bed. Mickey gained a dominant position and sat on my chest. His hands wrapped firmly around my throat. I saw how red his face was, and I realized he had lost control. I worried he thought I was someone else.

I didn't have any strength left to punch Mickey in the face or ribs. The battle for my life had come down to hand and finger strength. My hands were tired and sweaty, and as quickly as my fingers dislodged a couple of his from my neck, sweat caused them to slip. For about five seconds, I couldn't breathe or make any sounds. I became aware of some unusual street noise coming through the window, like ladies arguing in Spanish, and just as my eyes opened wide to listen, Mickey released his grip.

I quickly shoved him off me, ran down the stairs, and out of the apartment. I walked straight to Queens Boulevard and then a few more miles to the Long Island Expressway. I had no idea what was next for me, but I knew I didn't want to live with Mickey and my father anymore.

65

I hitchhiked the thirty miles out to Brentwood and walked toward the Healy's home on Grouse Drive. Thirsty, I was tempted to knock on someone's door to ask for a glass of water—or a drink from their garden hose. In the distance, I saw the Leigh brothers and some of my old friends who lived just a few houses from the Healys. They were throwing a football around and riding bikes. The whole scene was like a dream to me.

"So, did you go live with your family again?" my friend Steven asked.

"Yeah, for a while. It was OK, but I like it here better."

"Are you back at the Healys' again?"

"Well, that's what I'm hoping for. I ran away from my family. I'm afraid to knock on their door though."

"Why? They'll take you back." insisted Tommy Leigh.

"I don't know. What if they say they can't? What do I do then?"

My friend John offered, "Why don't you sleep at my house tonight?"

"Really? Your parents will let me?" I asked.

"Yeah man, they know you!" he assured me.

After going to John's house, his mother greeted me in their kitchen.

"Hi, Kevin! We missed you! Are you visiting the Healys?"

"Ah, tomorrow I will, I think."

She noticed my face and neck were red and scraped. "What happened to your face, Kevin? Did you get in a fight?"

"No, I was just wrestling with my brother."

"Oh, then where are your things?" she asked.

"They're in the city."

"Do your parents know you're here in Brentwood now?" she asked, now with some concern in her voice.

Rather than answer her question directly, I looked at the ground and fabricated an inordinately convoluted story about my current predicament. I could hear my friend John snickering as I spoke. His mother stood in front of me with her arms folded.

"So that's your story, Kevin?" she asked.

"Yeah."

The next morning, she dialed the Healy's number and briefly spoke with Margaret Healy before handing me the phone. Hearing Margaret Healy's voice gave me hope I might get back to a normal life again. I told her about what happened in Catskill, how I ran away to the city, how Mickey and I got into a big fight, and that I wasn't going to school anymore.

"Get back here now, Love! We will get this whole thing sorted out soon enough!" she assured me.

66

I really don't know who said what or how it was arranged, but within a few days, my situation did get straightened out—just like Margaret Healy said. I was fourteen years old and living at the Healys' again. I soon noticed Brentwood had changed considerably during the five months I was gone—or maybe I had grown up—and was able to notice a lot more than I had before. Peter and some of my friends had grown their hair long and taken up the hobbies of smoking pot and drinking beer. It all seemed like fun, like we weren't kids anymore and could do whatever we wanted to do.

I tried pot for the first time in the Healys' garage. Peter bought a nickel bag from a neighborhood kid. He even had his own pipe, a small metal device that screwed apart into several pieces so it could be cleaned. It was made *specifically* for smoking pot. He pinched some green, seedy pot out of the clear sandwich bag and loaded it into the bowl, which he lit with a match. He then took a hit, holding his breath for as long as he could.

I used the bottom of my T-shirt to wipe away the spit Peter left on the mouthpiece. I tentatively inhaled the hot smoke into my lungs—only to spastically cough it all out. The smoke was too hot for me. I eventually got the hang of it, and we smoked several bowls that night in the garage. I really wasn't sure whether I was high, but I certainly pretended to be. As long as I could say I tried it and I smoked pot too, such details didn't matter. I didn't want to get left behind. After a few nights of repeating the experience, I realized I was indeed getting high.

It wasn't long before I was hanging around with a group of kids who seemed to be drunk or high all the time. I started smoking all the pot and hashish anyone in the neighborhood would share. We raided our medicine cabinets—looking for Quaaludes, pain killers, diet pills, Valium, and anything else that might get us high. We even tried drugs without knowing for certain what they were for. It's possible that some of us took pills for gout or high blood pressure too.

We took various forms of LSD—all with names like blue microdot, window pane, blotter acid, or orange sunshine. We got the stuff from kids in the neighborhood, and if we couldn't get it from them, we bought it from other kids' older brothers or from anyone else who let it be known they had drugs for sale. There was always someone. We also drank beer, wine, and whiskey. And bourbon. And vodka.

67

To get money for beer and drugs, I started shoplifting albums and clothing from department stores. As my reputation for thievery developed, kids at school asked me to steal stuff for them. I made money by stealing anything from hockey sticks to stereos—and then selling it at a crazy discount. I discovered one way to steal was to nonchalantly carry things out of the store—unconcealed. I acted as though I already owned the stuff or had already paid for it. I got caught a couple of times and was almost caught many more.

On one occasion in tenth grade, I took some amphetamines in the morning and then realized I was in no condition to go to school. Instead, I rode my bike to a nearby mall. My goal was to steal several pairs of Levi's jeans from Macy's. I entered the changing room with the jeans I wanted and spent a while making sure they fit me. I decided not to follow my usual method of shoplifting and tried instead to conceal the jeans under my long winter coat. I packed them all as inconspicuously as I could and zipped my coat up. As I approached the double glass doors to leave the store, I saw a reflection of a man coming up fast behind me. I instinctively knew he was an undercover security guard.

I burst through the doors and out of the store, immediately dropping the jeans in the parking lot. I thought ditching the items might make the security guard stop.

I was wrong.

He continued to chase me—out of the parking lot and into the streets of the surrounding neighborhood. Fortunately, I was not only high on amphetamines but also in excellent physical condition. He was about thirty years old; I was fifteen. After a half-mile sprint, he got tired and leaned against a car. I stopped about fifty yards away and watched as he bent over to catch his breath. An hour or so later, I returned to the mall, picked up my bicycle, and went to school.

Stealing became my hobby. I stole dozens of ten-speed bicycles and sold them for twenty dollars each. Soon, any kid who had their bike stolen inevitably came looking for me. On one night, a guy who I knew from tenth grade saw me while I was loitering in front of the neighborhood liquor store—trying to get someone to buy beer for me. He had been left back a few times and was two years older than me. He was also much bigger and stronger than I was and easily pinned me up against the liquor store's front window.

"Where's my fucking bike, Weadock?" he bellowed.

"I didn't steal your bike, man!"

I may have been telling the truth. I had no idea where his bike was or whether I was the person who stole it. I stole a lot of bikes! He repeatedly pushed my chest, causing my back to slam against the large plate of glass each time. On one of the pushes, I heard the glass wobble. I became less focused on the hits to my chest and more focused on the glass behind me. I was afraid he was strong enough to push me through the window—or that the glass could pop out of its frame. I darted away into the night.

I don't know why, but the prospect of getting my ass kicked wasn't enough to stop me from stealing things. Peter and I and a few other wacked out kids tore up the neighborhood, frequently drunk or high on one drug or another. We stole street signs, speed-limit signs, stop signs, and any other signs we could remove with a wrench or screwdriver. We threw them in the nearest sewer or collected them in our bedroom. We threw eggs at houses and shot holes in neighbors' windows with BB guns. The Brentwood Public Library allowed anyone with a library card to sign out albums. We had no library card. We stole all the albums and sold them. We just wanted money to get high.

When Christmas came along, I stole stuff from Macy's to give away for gifts. I stole a triple-headed electric Norelco razor to give to Tom Healy. When he removed the wrapping paper, he immediately asked me where I got the money to buy it. I blathered on about saving money from work I did ... with a friend ... cleaning up backyards in the neighborhood ... on weekends ... last summer. I made it all up as I went along.

My answer was too convoluted for him to believe. With all of us sitting by the Christmas tree, and Christmas music playing in the background, he held the razor in his hand and lectured me on all the reasons why stealing was wrong. He also talked about why it was wrong to knowingly buy or accept stolen property. He then placed the razor by my feet and told me he didn't want it. He said if I didn't return it to Macy's—*he* would.

I had poisoned Christmas.

68

My friend Jimmy lived around the corner, and we spent many afternoons talking about karate, religion, girls, and cars. We spent a lot of time exercising together and laughing at jokes we made up about anything and everything under the sun. On one day, Jimmy borrowed his father's new car—a 1975 Plymouth Fury III. I sat up front while three other guys squeezed into the back seat. Jimmy was showing us how fast the car was, and drove sixty miles per hour through a narrow residential street. We were unaware the street had a small hill, which was about twenty-five feet from beginning to end and about six feet high. Jimmy unintentionally drove the car over it, and we instantly found ourselves airborne.

At the peak of our jump, I looked through the front windshield and saw a bunch of little children playing in the street on their plastic Big Wheel tricycles.

Miraculously, we missed everyone. The car hit the street so hard that the oil pan cracked and spilled its contents all over the asphalt. We rolled forty yards or so before stopping and getting out, only to have to face the shouting of the irate mothers and other residents. Like dogs with our tails between our legs, we pushed the car several miles back to Jimmy's house. As we approached Jimmy's house, I saw his father standing in his driveway with his arms folded. Only Jimmy had to face him. I walked home—like nothing happened.

My first attempt at driving a car came just a few days later. I got stoned one morning and drove some guy's car over 80 miles per hour down my own street—right past the Healy's house. Other guys drove at more than one hundred miles per hour—high on various combinations of hallucinogens and alcohol. A few died in these maniacal drives, usually by crashing into one of the many large pine trees that lined the main streets of Brentwood.

69

Tony lived with his father in a garden apartment complex; their unit was furnished with only their beds, a television, a folding table, and some accompanying folding chairs. They also had a cat and a litter box. Tony hung out with older guys who dropped out of high school years before. While hanging out with them one night, I witnessed a drug deal that became violent. I stood by and did nothing while someone stomped on the face of a guy who had sold Tony a hundred dollars of fake LSD. A bunch of the guy's front teeth, top and bottom, were loosened or knocked out, and his upper lip split halfway up to his nose. Afterward, he sat in the front seat of his new Trans Am, bleeding from his mouth and mumbling cries for help. He had previously boasted that he bought the car with the money he made from selling drugs. We just left him there. A few months later, one of the older guys was arrested for selling drugs and sentenced to a year in jail.

One morning, Tony woke me by knocking on my bedroom window. He had brought a pound of pot over to our house to cut up so he could sell it by the nickel bag, dime bag, and ounce. He promised to give Peter and me some pot if we would let him break it down in our bedroom. Within minutes, we were chopping the pot up, spreading it out on a piece of cardboard, and weighing portions out on a scale Tony stole from a science class. I had never seen so much of it! We smoked a few joints while listening to Black Sabbath—oblivious to the fact we should have been in school. Margaret Healy then burst into our room.

"What is that horrible smell?" she demanded. "And what is that stuff you've got there, Kevin?"

I didn't know what to say. We were busted.

"What *is* this?" she screamed.

"Pot ... marijuana," I admitted.

"Where did you get it?"

"Tony is holding it for some kid at school. He's gonna give it back to him today."

"And tell me now, why can't *that* kid hold it?"

I muttered, "I'm not sure, he just can't. I think he's in trouble with the cops."

"Get these drugs out of my house now, Kevin. *Now!*"

"OK, Mom, I will!"

Tony loaded everything into a plastic bag and stuffed it under his shirt. Margaret Healy escorted him off our property.

70

February nights can be brutally cold on Long Island. On one such night, the weather was far too cold for us to hang out on the streets—especially since some of us were getting ready to trip on LSD. Jimmy offered to let us all hang out in a fort his father built in his backyard. The fort had light, baseboard heat, and a few glass windows as well.

To reach the actual fort, we had to climb an eight-foot-high wooden ladder. Although the fort was built to hold three or four kids our size, five of us squeezed inside. A few of us took hits of acid and waited for the drug to take hold. I got tired of sitting and decided to stand. Another kid jokingly pushed me back, telling me to "Sit down, Weadock!"

In an attempt to maintain my balance, I extended my left arm to catch myself against the wall. However, my arm went through a window pane instead. After I pulled my arm back inside, I saw that I had a five-inch gash near my wrist. Blood sprayed everywhere, hitting everyone in the fort. Panicked, I pushed my way past the other kids and jumped off the top of the eight-foot ladder.

I ran into the night, with the wind blowing the blood that was pumping from the gash back into my face. The Healys' house was a quarter-mile away, and I was afraid I might bleed to death before I got there. When I entered the house, I could see long hot streams of blood squirting onto the walls of the stairwell that led up to the kitchen on the second floor.

I lunged onto a chair in the kitchen. The kitchen light let me see the clotted blood all over my body and clothing.

"I'm gonna die!" I yelled. "I'm gonna die! Help me! Help me! Help me!"

Anne ran into the kitchen first, followed by Margaret Healy, Eileen, and Peter. Margaret Healy dialed 911 and frantically told the dispatcher, "My son has cut his arm! He needs help. Please help us!"

None of us knew how to stop the bleeding. A huge pool of blood formed around me on the linoleum floor. I looked at the clock on the oven and noted the time was 9:34 p.m. I couldn't imagine still being alive by 10:00 p.m. I thought death might be good—I'd no longer have to experience the horror of bleeding to death.

Within a few minutes, Anne yelled that she saw red lights flashing against the front windows. Peter looked outside and said it was car number 302. Car 302 was from the Third Precinct in Suffolk County, and regularly patrolled our neighborhood. It just happened to be near our house when Margaret Healy dialed 911. Margaret Healy helped me get downstairs, out of the house, and into the back seat of the police car.

The officer drove at a high speed down Wicks Road toward South Side Hospital in Bay Shore. I glanced at the speedometer—we were going over eighty miles per hour. Blood continued to pump out of my wrist and onto the floor of the police car. The officer kept yelling over his shoulder, "Keep pressure on it!"

I tried doing that, but the blood continued to pour out around my hand—the gash was wider than my hand.

Sometime during the ride to the hospital, I apologized to Margaret Healy.

"I'm sorry, Mom," I murmured. "I know I've put you through a lot. I'm very sorry. I love you. You know that, right?" I had never told her before, but I felt like I had to. I sensed I might die that night.

Tearfully, she replied, "I know you love me—and I love you, too."

The policeman overheard our conversation, and tried to reassure us as we pulled up to the emergency room entrance. "Everything is going to be OK. The doctors will take care of you now."

Some hospital people pulled me out of the police car, put me on a stretcher, and rushed me into the emergency room. I could now feel the effects of the LSD I'd taken an hour before. The smell of alcohol wipes, the cold air conditioning, and all the beeping machines started to get to me. The nurses and doctors seemed to be speaking a foreign language. I couldn't tell where they ended—and the machines and drapes began. The noises and colors surrounding me blended into one signal to my brain, causing me to panic. As a nurse tried to keep me on the bed, I unintentionally kicked her in the chest.

A doctor came to her aid and injected me with something that calmed me down. He wrapped my wrist with gauze and stretched an ace bandage over it to stop the bleeding. He started examining the fingers on my injured hand and asked me a few questions.

"Can you feel my hand touching your fingers?"

"No," I answered.

"OK then, I want you to slowly make a fist now," he directed.

No matter how hard I tried to make a fist, my pinky and ulnar finger didn't move.

"Are you taking any drugs?" he asked. "We are going into surgery now, and the anesthesiologist needs to know."

"No, I'm not taking any drugs," I lied.

"If you're taking a drug we don't know about, the anesthesia might kill you. Do you understand?"

"I'm not taking any drugs. I swear!"

Margaret Healy was standing right there. I decided I'd rather die than let her know I had taken LSD.

In what seemed like less than five minutes, I was wheeled into the operating room. Someone put a mask on my face, knocking me out. I woke up sometime in the middle of the night. My arm was encased in a cast that extended to my fingers. Margaret and Tom Healy were by my side. Realizing I was still alive, and that they were there with me, produced an odd rush of warmth throughout my aching body.

I stayed in the hospital for several days. The only person from my family who came to visit me was Mickey. He hitchhiked from New York City just to see me. We hadn't seen each other since he tried to strangle me sixteen months earlier. He brought two joints with him, and I hid them in the space between the cast and my skin.

On the day I left the hospital, the surgeon who repaired my hand came into my room to talk to me. He told me the cast on my arm was stabilizing all the connections that had to be made again between severed nerves, arteries, veins, and tendons. He explained that because my ulnar nerve had been severed, I would never again have full feeling, strength, or movement in my left hand.

71

A few months after I injured my wrist, Mickey hitchhiked from the city to visit me at the Healys' again. Margaret and Tom Healy weren't home, so Peter, Mickey, and I hung out in the dining room and rummaged through their liquor cabinet. Mickey picked out an unopened quart of vodka and quickly gulped down half of it in less than a minute. Peter and I were amazed. We'd never seen anyone drink like *that*. Mickey got so drunk that he started wandering around outside the Healys' house and eventually passed out by a curb in front of my friend Jimmy's house.

When the police arrived, they tried to talk to Mickey, but he was incoherent—violently flailing, cursing, and crying. An ambulance soon showed up, and EMTs evaluated Mickey in front of a dozen or more neighbors. He had to be taken to the emergency room of a nearby hospital, where he was monitored and released late in the evening. When Margaret and Tom Healy got home, we told them what happened. It was a terrible thing for them to hear.

As though all this drama wasn't enough for the Healys, Dennis also came back to live with us. He had left my mother's house in Catskill and been placed in foster care again somewhere on Long Island. The Healys arranged to have him move back in with us. Just weeks after arriving, he and Peter got deep into a binge involving hard alcohol and LSD. Neither of them had bothered to go to school for weeks. They spent one notable afternoon drinking vodka and tripping on acid—eventually passing out on a neighbor's lawn. Seeing police cars and lights flashing just doors away, Margaret Healy walked outside to see what was happening. She was greeted by policemen who were unsure of what to do with the two kids they'd found collapsed in the grass, screaming in tongues, and soiled in their own vomit and urine.

"Oh, dear God!" Margaret Healy cried. "They're just like the bums of Brooklyn!"

Even I was embarrassed by the spectacle. I had never seen them so messed up before.

"How could they get so ossified, Kevin?"

"I don't know, Mom. They must have drank too much or something," I answered.

When the police tried to get the two boys off the neighbor's lawn, Dennis started screaming at everyone, including Margaret Healy. It was mostly slurred speech and gibberish, but the vulgarity came through for all to hear. A few weeks later, Dennis left the Healys' to live with Katie and her boyfriend in Catskill.

72

My mother and John moved from Catskill to a small town in Pennsylvania called Bath. They paid $5,000 for a small bungalow on a dirt road called Road #1. The bungalow was previously a hunting cabin—with an outhouse for a bathroom. Soon after moving in, they were able to have a healthy baby boy named Kristopher. Donna and Timmy also lived there, and Pat and Mickey drifted back and forth between living there or with my father in Jackson Heights. Pat and Mickey eventually converted a shed near the bungalow into a livable space. They used a five-gallon plastic bucket for a toilet and a kerosene heater to stay warm.

My mother and John lived paycheck to paycheck, and when John's monthly paycheck arrived in the mail, they filled the cabinets with food and then hit the bars with whatever money was left. Until the next paycheck came in, they just coasted, mostly sitting at the kitchen table, drinking beer, talking, and smoking cigarettes. My mother and John were difficult to be around when they were drunk. They fought violently, just like my mother and father had. Their fights also had exchanges of "motherfucker" and "cocksucker"—remarks all of us were familiar with from a prior version of the same life. During one of their fights, Mickey jumped in and hit John over the head with a cast-iron frying pan.

THE RIVER

During my first visit to the bungalow, I noticed Pat had many cuts on his wrists. There were dozens of them, each spaced about a quarter inch from one another and extending two to three inches perpendicular to the axis of his arm. Some had already turned into pink scars, others seemed like they were just made.

"Oh my God! What happened to your wrists, Pat?" I asked.

"Um, I don't really want to talk about it, Kevin."

"Well, was it a cat or a lawnmower or something?" I probed.

"I did it—it's too hard to explain, Kevin. Stop asking me about it!" he yelled back.

I didn't understand what had happened to my brother's mind. Whatever it was didn't matter to me. I still loved him as much as ever, but I wanted him to get back to normal.

Several weeks after I returned to the Healys', I received a call from Mickey. He told me Pat had tried to kill himself by turning off the oven's pilot light, turning on the gas, kneeling on the floor, and putting his head in the oven. Fortunately, the smell woke John, who turned the gas off and dragged Pat outside for fresh air. Mickey told me Pat was now locked up in a hospital's psychiatric ward.

After ending the call with Mickey, I felt helpless. I couldn't help Pat. I decided to write him a letter:

> *Dear Pat,*
> *Please don't kill yourself!*
> *We didn't even get a chance to be brothers again.*
> *Please promise me you won't try it again.*
> *Love, Kevin.*

I felt like I had to mail the letter immediately, so I walked toward the mailbox around the corner from our house. On the way, I passed a group of friends who were playing football in the street.

"Hey, where are you going, Weadock?"

"I have to mail this letter," I insisted.

One of them asked, "Hey, are you crying?"

I ran away before the other kids could see.

73

I asked the Healy's if I could visit Pat at the hospital. They gave me money to take the trip—a train to New York followed by a bus out to Easton, Pennsylvania. My mother and John picked me up at the bus station just as it started to get dark and drove me straight to the hospital.

We took an elevator up a few floors to the psychiatric ward and rang the buzzer that was outside a set of heavy metal doors with wire reinforced windows. A nurse let us in and told us to wait by the nurse's station. Moments later, another set of metal doors opened to the room and Pat entered, wearing just a wrinkled white T-shirt and baggy pants. He was pale and had perspiration on his forehead. I was rattled by how skinny he was now—with cheekbones, jaw, and elbows all pressing out against his skin.

"Hi Pat ... are you OK?" I asked in desperation.

"Yeah, I'm OK Kevin. They're taking good care of me here, so please don't worry. Alright?"

"OK, but when are you getting out?" I asked.

"In about a week or two, I think," he assured me.

After just ten minutes or so, the nurse took him back behind the metal doors.

74

In attempts to avoid getting my ass kicked or possibly arrested for any number of things, I ran away from the Healys' many times. After a night in a cell at Suffolk County's third precinct—the result of being arrested for "acting in concert to harass," running away when things got tough became a soft option for me. I didn't want to ever put Tom Healy in the position of having to bail me out of jail again.

Sometimes I ran away to be with Katie, who was living in Catskill. She usually shared an apartment with a boyfriend or a friend or two. I felt safe with her and I didn't have to explain why I was there. In fact, I showed up without notice. It didn't matter to her anyway—she was just happy to see me. I'd stay with her for a couple of days before hitchhiking to my father's apartment in Jackson Heights or my mother's bungalow in Pennsylvania. Sometimes Pat and Mickey were there—sometimes they were in a halfway house in Allentown—or jail. Dennis was running away from rough situations too, and we occasionally met up in Jackson Heights, Catskill, or Pennsylvania. I didn't know who would be where until I got there.

During one of my escapes to Jackson Heights, Mickey asked me to walk with him to a barber shop on Broadway in Elmhurst.

THE RIVER

"Are you getting a haircut?" I asked.

"Nah, I just have to talk to the guy about something."

When we entered the barber shop, only a thin older man with a bald head stood near the back of the shop. He seemed nervous or bothered about something.

While staring at me, he asked Mickey, "Who's this?"

"This is my brother, Kevin."

"How come I never heard about him?" asked the barber.

"I don't know. He lives on Long Island—that's probably why."

"OK Mick, you're driving me crazy. Let's see what you got."

We walked into a tiny room just behind where the barber chairs were. Mickey then pulled a tightly folded paper bag out from under his shirt and put it on a small desk. The barber then briefly examined a revolver and pistol that he pulled from the bag.

"Not bad, Mick. Not bad at all," the barber said, almost in a whisper.

He put the guns into a small duffle bag and handed Mickey some cash. After leaving the barber shop, we walked back to Jackson Heights. I knew better than to ask Mickey how he got the guns.

Where I went to when I ran away didn't really matter. I only wanted to put control of my life back into *my* hands—or so I thought. I even spent a couple of days at a house where some guys from a motorcycle gang lived. I'd usually stay gone for a week or so, causing Margaret and Tom Healy a great deal of stress—but they always forgave me.

Tom Healy spent many nights at the kitchen table trying to talk sense into me. He patiently listened to all my cockeyed reasons for doing the things I did. In return, he spoke about what was right and what was wrong and how I could have handled situations differently. As he spoke, Margaret Healy listened in with her eyes wide open, staring at my face to see whether anything was sinking in. She moved about the kitchen, ready to contribute little phrases of her own.

"That's right, Tommy."

"Can't you see that, Kevin?"

Her arthritic hip caused her to limp while she paced back and forth between the refrigerator and stove. She was on the lookout for anything she could do to help Tom Healy communicate to me. She kept his cup of tea full, emptied his ashtray, and occasionally placed a piece of coconut custard or mince pie down in front of him. I usually just let his advice go in one ear and out the other. Maybe a sentence or two would register one night, maybe half a sentence the next.

Eileen had steered completely clear of all the insanity Peter and I were involved in, but she walked through the kitchen at times just to hear about our antics. Occasionally, she listened in from the living room, and I heard her giggling and commenting.

"Oh Lord!"

"Dear God!"

"My word!"

Eileen suffered from lupus, a disease that kept her weak and in chronic pain. She didn't attend much of tenth or eleventh grade and had to be tutored at home. I think some part of her lived vicariously through Peter and me.

75

Although our initial venture into drugs and alcohol was based on a desire to fit in, be cool, and have fun, it evolved into something else for Peter and me. All the crime, drug use, and drunkenness eventually took its toll. Some of the trips I had taken on LSD were so frightening that I feared I would never be sane again.

Still—it was better to be high than it was to be thinking about our *real* lives. I was suspended seven times in tenth grade and five times in the first half of eleventh grade. Our friendships with other kids faded. We had no hobbies or accomplishments to speak of, just afternoon upon afternoon and night after night of intoxication, masturbation, and sleep. We rarely brushed our teeth or showered. Margaret Healy frequently tried to get us out of bed earlier in the day by rattling our bedroom door or pulling our blankets off us. When we did get up and go to the kitchen for food, we were greeted with her sardonic version of Matthew 27:53; "Well ..., the dead have arose and appeared to many."

Peter decided to drop out of high school. He stopped leaving the house and even avoided looking out the windows. Inside his head was a world of fear and hopelessness. I didn't know how to reach him anymore. One day, I spent about 30 minutes coaxing him out of a closet.

I sometimes wanted to call my mother in Pennsylvania and speak to her or Pat about how I was feeling. However, I didn't want Margaret Healy to know I was calling my mother, so I walked a couple of blocks to use a pay phone outside a gas station. I called my mother "collect," knowing she usually accepted the charges. She was usually so drunk that I just hung up the phone. The same thing happened when I tried to speak with Pat—he was drunk and incoherent. I tried calling at different times of the day too, but with the same result. After a while, I stopped walking to the gas station.

Pat evidently felt bad about not being able to speak coherently with me and decided to call me at the Healys'. He asked me to hitchhike into the city and meet him at our father's apartment in Jackson Heights. When I got there, Pat and I decided to take a walk around the neighborhood. While we were walking, I told him I was confused about so many things in my life and that I felt nervous and depressed. He was like a guru to me, steering our conversation toward subjects such as meditation and psychology and philosophy. He read a lot on those topics, and I loved listening to him talk about them. I could tell he had experienced the same feelings I was struggling with. As we continued to walk, we talked about all sorts of things—our family, girls, mathematics, the Beatles, Bob Dylan, Sigmund Freud, and anything else that came to mind. He even told me he recently had sex with a girl. He said the most amazing thing about the experience was that "she loved me back."

I started feeling hopeful that, with Pat's guidance, I could find my way out of being depressed. At one point in our walk, Pat decided he wanted to buy beer. He went into a deli and bought a six-pack of sixteen-ounce Budweiser

THE RIVER

cans. I took one and started to drink it as we sat on a bench just outside the Elmhurst Avenue subway station. Pat also took one, but instead of drinking at a normal pace, he guzzled it down. He did the same for the next four beers, all before I finished my first. He eventually passed out, right beside the deli where we bought the beer.

76

Every time I ran away, I missed a week or two of school. When I *did* go to school, I was drunk, stoned, or both. I really didn't care about anything that was happening there. If I was too high to walk the halls, the school nurse let me sleep it off in her office. This led to detentions, suspensions, and failed classes.

Detention involved sitting in the library for an hour after school ended. I sat by a window that allowed me to watch the other kids as they boarded buses to go home. I passed the time by reading some books which were on the bookshelf closest to me. They happened to be books about psychology, and one was called *A Primer of Freudian Psychology*. Pat had told me about Sigmund Freud. I was curious to learn more, so I started reading. I loved learning about the id, ego, and superego!

I hoped the information in the books would help me feel better. I especially loved reading a book called *Abnormal Psychology*. I was somehow comforted when I recognized the names of students who had previously signed the book out. *Abnormal Psychology* explained topics such as the different types of schizophrenia, manic depression, psychosis, and neurosis. Reading it was a double-edged sword—I loved learning about mental illness, but I also worried I had some of the disorders.

THE RIVER

One night, I saw Tom Healy sitting by himself at the kitchen table, working on "the figures" again. I walked in and sat at the table with him.

"Well, if it isn't himself!" he said with a smile.

"What's on your mind?" he asked.

I told him about the psychology books I was reading at school—and that *I* wanted to talk to a psychologist. He was shocked by my announcement.

"I know you're going through a tough period in your life now, Kevin, but I don't think you need to see a *psychologist!*"

"I think I do, Dad. I'm more messed up than you know. Do you want to hear about it?"

"Yes, let me hear it," he agreed.

He lit up a cigarette and leaned back from the table to listen. I told him everything. I explained how depressed I was; how much alcohol I drank; how many drugs I was taking; how I wasn't going to school; and how I had been vandalizing the houses, schools, libraries, factories, and stores nearby. After hearing the full extent of what my life had become, he encouraged me to ask my social worker to get me to a psychologist.

77

Tom Mooney was a hippie with long brown hair and a beard. He wore sandals and drove an old VW van. Margaret Healy fed him dinner every time he came over to see me, which was about once a week. He was funny and kind. He tried to bond with me—and often succeeded. I told him about my conversation with Tom Healy, and he agreed to make an appointment for me to see a psychologist named Dr. D'Amato. He said the psychologist specialized in treating kids my age.

I couldn't believe I was *finally* going to be able to talk to a psychologist. I thought about all the things I wanted to discuss—but then quickly changed my mind, deciding that telling him *everything* wasn't such a good idea. Maybe I'd just tell him a little bit the first day so he didn't think I was weird. I was also worried that some of the stuff I wanted to talk about might get me into trouble with the police.

I first went to see the psychologist on a cold and overcast afternoon. I anxiously rode my bike the five miles there and locked it up outside a small two-story brick building. The office of Raymond D'Amato, PhD, was on the second floor. His secretary told me to wait in a chair by the water cooler. I squirmed in my seat, looked at the clock, stretched—whatever I could do to keep myself together. Eventually, Dr. D'Amato walked out of his office and introduced himself. I was amazed to have someone so smart, an actual doctor, extending his hand to shake mine. I followed him into his office, which was just slightly larger than his desk. The window in his office faced the busy Wicks Road, and the sound of cars and trucks zooming by permeated the glass.

Dr. D'Amato was in his late thirties and had brown hair and glasses. He wore a suit and tie, but left the jacket hanging on the wall.

"Please sit down," he said in a friendly tone.

"So, what brings you here today?" he asked.

"I think I'm depressed or something. I don't know what it is. I don't know how to get back to being happy. I'm pretty messed up, I think—I'm not sure."

He smiled back at me. "Tell me a little about yourself, Kevin. How old you are, where you're from, stuff like that."

"Well, I'm sixteen years old and I was born in Brooklyn—but then I moved to Rockaway Beach and some other places. It's hard to explain."

"And your family? Tell me a little about them."

"Oh, boy—my family is messed up. I'm actually in a foster home right now."

"What does *messed up* mean, Kevin?"

"Well, we got split up when I was eight years old, and both of my parents are alcoholics, and they're divorced. Well, actually, they never got married—and we had to live in The Shelter and stuff. It's a long story."

"So, are *you* messed up, Kevin?"

"Probably. I mean, I feel messed up."

"*How* are you messed up, Kevin?"

In just minutes, I was in full gear. I told him I got drunk or high on drugs every day for the past two years. I told him I was stealing things like bicycles and clothing and whatever else I wanted. I told him I barely went to school anymore and I had been suspended many times. I told him my left hand was badly injured and I couldn't use it or feel anything with it anymore. I told him about running away and fighting and feeling like I was totally lost. I told him I felt horrible about how my behavior was affecting my foster parents. And then I had to explain the whole stupid story about being a foster kid. And my life. And how much I missed my brothers and sisters.

Once I started crying, I wasn't sure how I could stop—or whether I should stop—or just let the outburst run its course.

Dr. D'Amato placed a box of tissues near me and remained quiet. When I stopped crying, he remarked, "I'm sorry you've had these things happen in your life. I really am." He said it was great that I shared my thoughts and feelings with him, and that it would eventually help me feel better.

Before I knew it, the session was over. I rode my bike back home with puffy eyes and a new sense of hope. I couldn't wait for the next session.

78

My weekly appointments with Dr. D'Amato lasted forty-five minutes each. They seemed to go by too quickly. I could have easily stayed for twice as long. I loved talking about my problems and getting feedback that might help me feel better. I cried in many of the sessions, sometimes so deeply that I felt like I was wailing. A few times, I worried I had lost control of myself.

As the sessions went on, I realized I was still mourning the loss of time with my siblings—I could never get it back. This grief was most painful when I thought about losing Donna and Timmy from my life. I remembered what cute little babies they were, and how much my siblings and I adored them. Timmy turned two years old just days before we went to live at The Shelter. Donna was only four years old. I never really lived with them again after that day. As I got older, I didn't give the loss much conscious thought. But it was there all along, simmering in my unconscious mind.

I also told Dr. D'Amato that I wondered whether I was lovable, whether I was worth fighting for. I never had a good explanation for why my parents left me at The Shelter, Little Flower, and the Watermans' for so long. I was stuck on the notion that maybe there was something about *me* that made them leave me in those places. Or maybe I just didn't matter to them. In a way, I really didn't want to know the answers to these questions.

I also spoke with Dr. D'Amato about being a foster kid. I told him I had a hard time explaining my situation and introducing myself to others. The word "foster" was like an asterisk next to my name and identity. I felt like I wasn't whole or equal to kids in "normal" homes.

I talked about how I couldn't see myself ever being able to have a girlfriend. I couldn't imagine anyone ever wanting to fall in love with me. In my mind, anyone who could fall in love with me must have something wrong with them.

One session ended early after I spoke with Dr. D'Amato about the four times I had been hospitalized; once for 4 days and three other times for a week each. I was embarrassed to tell him that my parents never came to visit me there. I clamped up. I just wanted to get on my bike and ride home.

I felt horrible during many of my bicycle rides back home. I unpacked a lot of emotional stuff in Dr. D'Amato's office, stuff that was still unresolved—half in, half out. The pain and fear I stirred up in some sessions haunted me, and I wondered if I should stop talking to him. But after a few days, I felt better and was ready for the next session. I soon committed myself to sticking with Dr. D'Amato. I never missed a session, even if I was sick or had to ride my bike five miles in the rain or against a freezing wind. I always went.

At the beginning of one session, Dr. D'Amato surprised me with a simple question: "Kevin, tell me what you want your future to look like?"

THE RIVER

I drew a blank. I couldn't think of anything to say. I had never really thought about it. I had only assumed a steady decline toward the same type of life my parents had.

"I don't know," I finally declared. "I just don't want to get in any more trouble, I guess."

"What would your life look like, Kevin—if *you* had the power to make it come true?"

After a long pause, I found the courage to say what I really wanted: "I'd like to be married to someone."

"That's a wonderful thing to think about, Kevin. What else?"

"They would have to love me back," I added.

"Well, why wouldn't they?"

"I don't know," I muttered, looking out the window.

"What else would your life look like—if *you* could make it come true?"

"I'd like to have a couple of kids and a good job and a house. And I want to live by the ocean ... or in the city."

"Seems like that would be a wonderful life, Kevin!"

"Yeah, I guess so."

"Well, I see no reason why these things can't be part of your life. Do you?"

"I guess so. I mean, I hope so. I don't know."

After a few months of seeing Dr. D'Amato, I stopped drinking hard alcohol and stopped taking LSD, mescaline, and other drugs. I also stopped shoplifting and vandalizing the neighborhood.

79

I rode my bicycle on a street that was lined on both sides with tall pine trees. The blue sky stretched beyond the treetops, and a warm summer breeze blew against my face. I was watching out for cars and people—but became more and more mindful of how beautiful the day was. The green pines nearby, the blue sky, the smell of flowers, the sound of birds, and the warm air I was cutting through—they were all just so perfect.

The moment precipitated a flashback to the beautiful day I had as a child in Minnesota—the day at the Gibsons' house, when I watched my family through the window of a bedroom perched high above them. The memory was a connection to a part of myself that was solid, a part that had survived the chaos of the last ten years. I again saw that life can be beautiful, and that good things can be had and felt. I locked-in on the emotional structure of what I was now feeling, with the hope I could use it as a guiding light, a positive view of my future. I told myself—don't forget this moment!

As the fog of drug use and depression disappeared, I started seeing parts of my life I had almost forgotten. I was lying in my bed one day, skipping out of school, when I started thinking about my sister Anne—who was now seven years old. Although I had been living with her for six years, I really didn't know her that well. I was a horrible brother! I felt an urgent need to do something about it.

I quickly rode my bicycle to her school. I rode along the perimeter of the building, peering into the windows of one classroom after another, until I saw kids that were approximately Anne's age. I eventually spotted her, sitting at her desk in the back of a classroom. To get her attention, I called her name and frantically waved my arms above my head. Although initially embarrassed by my behavior, she eventually began to smile. I became mindful of her cute little face, and it dawned on me that she looked just like Mickey—dark hair, big brown eyes, high cheekbones—and just a few freckles. I wondered how I hadn't noticed the resemblance before.

Anne's classmates became distracted when they saw me, causing the teacher to rush over to the window and shoo me away with dramatic waves of her hand. I rode my bike away from the window and into the parking lot, where I rode in circles of varying diameters between all the parked cars until the school day ended. Several months earlier I would have been looking in the cars for things to steal! But I was different now—those days were gone. As Anne waited in line to get on her school bus, I rode my bike right up to her.

"Hi, Anne!"

She was blushing—but still happy I was there.

"What are *you* doing here?" she asked.

"I just wanted to see you... to say hello," I told her.

"You're *so* weird!" she kidded, rolling her eyes and shaking her head before scurrying up the school bus steps.

80

I eventually started getting interested in school again. Sometime during the third quarter of eleventh grade, I asked my English teacher, Mr. Monday, if it was possible for me to catch up with the rest of the class. He was happy to hear me ask him that question; however, he shocked me by stating that catching up would be almost impossible. I'd have to read six books in the next month. I had no idea I was *that* far behind!

I started on a nonstop reading frenzy of books such as *The Catcher in the Rye*, *1984*, *Moby Dick*, *Marathon Man*, and *One Flew Over the Cuckoo's Nest*. I had to write book reports as well, one after the other. Reading books and writing reports were the first things I did when I came home from school. Mr. Monday was so happy with my efforts that he started coming over to the Healys' house once a week to help me. By the end of eleventh grade, I had caught up to the rest of the class.

My teachers in high school were all aware of what I was trying to do with myself, and they worked with me to help me catch up. My shop teacher, Mr. Izzo, frequently asked me to play tennis with him after school. He talked to me while we worked in the shop and played tennis, and he tried to give me advice on everything he could. Because I had not taken algebra, biology, chemistry, or physics, the principal and other teachers made a "special case" for me to have shop classes serve as credits in place of the other required courses so I could graduate on time.

In twelfth grade, I didn't even bother trying to catch the bus to school. Instead, I hitchhiked there each morning. I basically had my own schedule—my day started whenever I got there. I worked on shop projects or caught up with whatever assignments my teachers had given me.

After school, I worked at a Chinese restaurant called Fung Young House. I washed dishes, pots, and tea cups by hand. I cut onions, made rice, mopped floors, emptied garbage, cleaned bathrooms, and did anything else they asked me to. I was working about thirty hours per week at two dollars per hour. The job not only put money in my pocket but also kept me out of trouble at night. The Chinese guys liked me because I worked as hard as they did. They showed me how to cook on a wok and enjoyed having me taste *real* Chinese food. I helped them with their English, and they made sure I was nearby when the results of horse races at Aqueduct were broadcast over the radio.

Toward the time when my teachers thought I might graduate, I went to my guidance counselor for some "mandatory" advice on what I should do for my future career. I had never seen him before and didn't even know his name.

"Well, let's see here," he said as he glanced over my paperwork. "Have you given much thought to what you might want to do after high school?"

I admitted, "No, not really. I might try to travel to California if I can save some money. I don't know, really."

"Any careers or jobs you think you might want to pursue after that?"

"Not really, maybe a police officer or a psychologist. I don't know. What do you think I should do?"

"Have you ever thought of animal husbandry?"

"What's that?" I wondered.

He explained, "It's a career where you wash and feed horses and other farm animals, like goats and pigs."

****

While I had done enough to graduate, my overall GPA was dismal, and I graduated at the bottom of my class. That detail really didn't matter to me. I was amazed I had graduated from high school. I was the first in my family to do so. I even got invited to a graduation party, at which I got to hang out with all the popular kids. They had cars and girlfriends and talked about which colleges they were going to. The few people who *did* know my name only knew me as a punk or a stoner and were surprised to see me. I left the party after fifteen minutes without saying goodbye to anyone, even the kid who invited me.

About a week after I graduated, I was in my room with Peter when we heard our dog Smokey barking. Margaret Healy called down to us from upstairs, telling me that "some girl" was at the front door—asking for *me*!

In my mind, the scenario was virtually impossible. I was extremely shy around girls. I rarely spoke to them and had never had anything close to a girlfriend. Why would a girl be looking for *me*? When I walked upstairs to the door, I saw a girl I knew from the park where I drank beer and listened to music with friends. Her name was Carol. She was a freckle-faced girl who had graduated with me. I opened the door and poked my head out, keeping my feet inside the house.

"Hi, Carol," I said.

She didn't live in my neighborhood, so I thought she was going to ask me a simple question like, "Do you know where so-and-so lives?"

From the kitchen, Margaret Healy's voice chimed, "Are you going to let her in, or what?"

Carol stepped into our house.

Frozen, I said nothing.

"Hi, Kevin. I'm headed up to the park. Wanna come?"

Before I could think of an excuse for why I couldn't walk with her, Margaret Healy, who was suddenly peering down at us from the top of the stairs, jumped into the conversation.

"Yes, he does," she insisted. "Don't you, Kevin?"

81

Tom Mooney showed up one afternoon in mid-August to speak with Margaret Healy. As usual, he sat at our kitchen table and ate the dinner Margaret Healy had prepared for him.

Margaret Healy soon called for me to join them.

"Kevin, come here, Love," she said. "Tom wants to speak with you about something very important."

I sat down at the kitchen table and leaned forward to listen.

He began, "Kevin, whether you know it or not, you are officially a ward of New York State, which makes you eligible for a program called the Equal Opportunity Program."

"Uh huh," I mumbled, trying to get a sense of what his point was.

"If I can get you into this program, you can go to a community college for a year and take all the courses you missed in high school. And since you're a ward of the state, it's all paid for."

"Well, I already graduated high school, so why bother?"

"Well, if you take these courses and get a B average, they will let you into a community college anywhere in New York State for free. You'll have to take a year of algebra, chemistry, biology, and so on, but these credits won't be college credits."

"Where do I have to go to do this?"

"The State University of New York at Farmingdale. It's a two-year school about fifteen miles from here. They'll pay for room, board, tuition, books, and give you $500 per semester to live there too!"

Margaret Healy was smiling at me. "I'm sure Kevin will do it, Tom!" she exclaimed. "Won't you, Love?"

"I guess," I agreed. "But when does it start?"

"Two weeks. It starts in two weeks," said Tom Mooney.

"OK, I'll try it. It beats washing dishes," I said.

Tom Mooney had brought a stack of financial aid forms with him, in case I wanted to get into the program. I just put a zero in every row that asked me about my income and assets.

"And don't forget to write 'Ward of New York State' on the top of every page," Tom Mooney instructed.

Two weeks later, I was almost eighteen years old and on my way to college. The official name of the program was Developmental Studies. I took pride in telling all my friends I was going to college.

"My major is just like liberal arts," I told them.

82

Tom Mooney brought me to the campus, wished me luck, and drove away. I carried two shopping bags full of my clothes, sheets, and pillow cases around the campus until I found my dormitory. I made my bed and sat there for a while, not sure what I should do next. Within a few hours, I was hanging around with other students, drinking beer, listening to music, and throwing a frisbee in front of the building.

Later that night, I went to my room and laid on my bed, staring at the ceiling. The smell of cleaning agents and the "institutional" feel of the dormitory reminded me of my first day at The Shelter. I started thinking about how I felt on that first day—about the lady who gave me the blue socks, and the lady who yelled at my brother Paddy for drinking milk out of the container, and how my parents just walked away, and ... "fight night." My heart started beating rapidly, and I just didn't understand how old feelings could come back like that. I didn't know how to make the anxious feeling go away. I made the situation worse by suspecting something nefarious was taking place—that someone had secretly put LSD in my beer. I had heard stories like that from other kids, so the same could've been happening to me. I ran out of the dorm, screaming to people who were walking around the campus that someone had secretly given me LSD and that I was "freaking out!"

Some kid told me to go to the infirmary, where I could speak with the campus nurse. I ran there and pounded on the door. A soft-spoken nurse, probably about sixty years old, invited me to come inside. I tried unsuccessfully to explain what was happening to me. She called my dorm counselor and asked her to come talk to me.

Within a few minutes, a young woman named Lorraine showed up. She had long wavy hair and was wearing beads, sandals, bell-bottoms, and a tie-dye shirt. To help me get my mind off my self-induced hysteria, she asked me where I was from, what I was studying, and what kind of music I liked. After many hours of talking about dozens of topics, we left the infirmary. We walked back to the dorm just as the sun was coming up, and I went to my room and fell asleep.

I had another panic attack during my first class at college. I ran out of the classroom and back to the dorm to speak with Lorraine again. She again asked me about many random subjects, all unrelated to school or my life. We talked for hours about music and sports and psychology—anything but topics related to panicking! These emergency meetings with Lorraine occurred several more times over the following weeks—yet I remained afraid I might freak out again.

I began drinking beer more frequently—and in greater amounts. I didn't care what anyone else thought about my constant drinking. When a student in my dorm asked me why I was drinking beer before lunch, I promptly replied with Dorothy Parker's famous line, "*I'd rather have a bottle in front of me than a frontal lobotomy.*"

I wasn't kidding. It was more important to me to bury the panic with alcohol. I couldn't make it through a day without it. This level of drinking resulted in monstrous hangovers that made me swear to myself I would never drink again. It didn't matter. I'd start drinking again that same day—just as soon as I feared I might have a panic attack. Although I went to all my classes and studied in the library at night, I was unable to hold my hands out in front of me without them shaking. I deliberately hid them in my pockets so other people couldn't see the tremor.

I feared this whole experience was my portal to alcoholism. I decided to go to the campus psychologist to talk about the panic attacks and my growing dependence on alcohol. He surprised me with his reaction.

"Why don't you have a panic attack right here, right now?" he challenged.

I tried to replicate the thought process that initiated the attacks, but I just couldn't do it.

He helped me realize that the *fear* was driving the fear, and that if I didn't fear the fear, I wouldn't have a panic attack. He said I should "allow the fear to come," and I should "let it run its course through my body and mind." That was easier said than done, but the advice helped me a great deal. After that session, no one knew better than I did about the meaning of FDR's famous words, "*The only thing we have to fear is fear itself.*"

83

I wasn't even drunk! I don't know what the guy said or did, but it was certainly enough to trigger a fight. Dozens of students gathered around to watch us roll around on the lawn of the campus library. We exchanged punches and head-locks and other moves used by people who don't *really* know how to fight. When the fight was over, I went into the library and studied.

On another day, I was angry at a member of the Farmingdale lacrosse team because I thought he said something about me while I stood in line in the cafeteria. After lunch, I walked directly to his dorm room to confront him. To my surprise, three other guys were hanging out with him in his room. He was equally surprised to see me there.

"Let's go, motherfucker!" I yelled.

"I have no idea who you are, dude!" he insisted, laughing along with his friends. "I have no fucking idea what you're talking about or why you're here!"

Several days later, I fought another guy during a party in my dormitory. The fight caused us both to crash through the window in the lobby. I spent much of that night in a hospital emergency room and had to have several small lacerations on my arms stitched up. Lorraine picked me up from the hospital. I sat in her front passenger seat. I had nothing to say—I knew my days at college were numbered.

Due to these events, Lorraine spent a lot of time with me in her apartment, which had colorful tapestries hanging on the walls and candles and incense burning from a small table in the center of her living room. We talked and drank herbal tea for hours. Usually, some Grateful Dead, Janis Joplin, or Neil Young music played in the background. I told Lorraine about my past and how the look, feel, and smell of the dormitory reminded me of living in The Shelter. I told her I'd rather get my ass kicked than back down from someone—because if I *did* back down, I'd be giving the other person power over me. I told her about my life at the Waterman home and how I would never let anyone have that kind of power over me again. They would have to kill me first.

Lorraine helped me see that the trauma I experienced as a kid was in some way playing out in college; I needed to understand that not every conflict or disagreement had to be settled by fighting. She warned me that my stay on campus was in jeopardy and that I needed to focus more on my courses and spend less time getting drunk. She also encouraged me to keep seeing the school psychologist, which I did. I also hitchhiked back to Brentwood to continue my sessions with Dr. D'Amato.

Despite having two psychologists *and* Lorraine helping me adjust to college life, I was still afraid that I wasn't going to survive on my own. I wrote a long list of positive personal affirmations down on a piece of paper and carried it around in my wallet. I looked at the list whenever I needed to. I also hitchhiked into Manhattan a few times to try my luck at prayer in St. Patrick's Cathedral.

84

I worked on my class notes every day, taking as many as I could during lectures and then copying them over into a separate notebook I used to study from. Doing well in my classes became the singular focus in my life. Getting good grades became a source of self-esteem for me. I also started to develop a wonderful social life. I made many new friends and went to countless parties.

Being at college enabled me to think about my life in ways I hadn't before. I thought about how messed up my childhood had been, and I started having unusually long, wailing cries at night. Some of them seemed to be out of my control—I couldn't stop them once they started. The episodes were all about grief and loss, especially loss of time with my siblings. I felt horrible they didn't get the love and support they deserved. I felt guilty they weren't in college too. I thought about how much I loved them all and how badly they had been hurt by our experience. It was bottomless sorrow.

Nonetheless, I felt the crying sessions were healing me. I envisioned a large knot of neurons had formed in my brain over the years and that the dense, convoluted network reflected my complicated emotions. The network of neurons couldn't produce a coherent thought—it could only drive my significant crying episodes. My roommate was empathetic and, to my knowledge, didn't tell anyone else I cried at night.

After a while, I became tired of crying. I was making great bonds with so many people and wanted to feel all the joy they brought to my life. I decided I needed to distance myself from my family until I was done with school. I impulsively grabbed a shoebox that held all the letters and photographs I had ever collected from my family and threw it in a garbage can in the lobby of my dorm. Before throwing it out, I was tempted to look at everything one last time. I thought maybe certain letters or pictures should *never* be thrown out. But I didn't look—I just threw them all out.

The next morning, I went to retrieve the letters and photographs from the garbage, but someone had already emptied the can.

85

It was an old brownstone building somewhere in New York City. I walked up a darkened wooden stairway, up to a mahogany-stained wooden door on the second floor. I opened the door and walked into a darkened movie theater. On the walls, off in the distance, were small stained-glass windows that provided just enough light for me to see a long set of stairs that led down to the picture screen. I walked down the stairs and stopped just a few rows from the screen, which was showing a panoramic Technicolor view of a real river on a hot sunny day.

With full noise and smell, the river flowed at a fast pace from my right to my left. The river was swollen and moved just like any large river moves after a major storm. Thousands of bodies filled the water. Many were dead. Some were almost dead. Many rotting body parts floated by as well, twisting and bobbing with the current. Flocks of raucous birds flew above, occasionally diving into the water to feed. The people who were still alive moaned as they looked or reached toward the bank of the river for someone to pull them to safety.

I wanted to rescue the living people from the river, so I took the remaining few steps down to the screen, which had become the edge of the river itself. I could clearly see some of the faces of the people floating past, many with flesh peeling off their bodies. Legs stuck out of the water at various angles, tumbling and sinking as the river roared by. I recognized a few people I had known or seen in my life. There was the one-legged black man who

I had stared at years before as he lay next to a garbage can in Hell's Kitchen. Drunk, he had fallen off his wheelchair and into a pool of his own urine, his pants down below his waist and his penis exposed. I remembered thinking it would be hard to get any lower in life than that. I also saw the decapitated head of a redheaded kid I knew from high school. He had destroyed his mind by taking LSD too many times and ended up being committed to Pilgrim State Psychiatric Center. He stared at the sky above as the river caused his head to spin.

I then saw my mother in the river. An eddy in the river pushed her closer to me, with her head and torso above the water. She was still alive, exhausted, and moaning. She extended her arm across a rotting corpse, hoping I could grab her hand. I reached down and grabbed her wrist. I felt the weight of her body and the drag of the river on the corpse between us. Other bodies were bumping into her as well, and I feared the skin on her arms might peel off while I held her. I eventually pulled her closer so the top part of her body was in the theater with me. I couldn't see where her legs were or whether she still had them. In a desperate, crying voice, she told me there was no chance for her. She said I needed to do what I had to do and that she loved me no matter what. She then slipped from my grip and fell back into the river, drifting away with all the other dead and dying people.

86

Graduating from the one-year Developmental Studies program was a big deal for me. I felt I had caught up to where I should have been when I graduated high school. Unfortunately, the Healys moved to Wilmington, Delaware, just as I finished the program. I stayed in Brentwood and lived in my friend Jimmy's basement. I worked as a porter in a nearby factory, and I hitchhiked on the Long Island Expressway to Farmingdale after work to take two courses at night. I got out of class at 10:00 p.m., and I still had to hitchhike back to Jimmy's house. That summer, I chose medical laboratory technology for my major. As usual, I filled out all the financial forms with zeros and wrote "Ward of New York State" on the top of each page.

Medical laboratory technology was an intense two-year program consisting of courses in hematology, renal physiology, urinalysis, parasitology, and clinical chemistry. I developed my own study method that involved trying to answer all the questions at the end of every chapter in the textbook, whether we covered them in class or not. If I still didn't understand something, I'd hunt down my closest friend and study partner, Billy McNally. A couple years before Billy started at SUNY Farmingdale, his spine had been severely injured. He was permanently confined to a wheelchair. I barely noticed it. Between the two of us, we could figure out almost anything.

Neither of us had any *real* money. Billy and I played foosball together in the campus bar, and when we needed a drink, Billy wrote a check for a pitcher of beer, usually just three dollars. In an attempt to end our financial misery, we often went to a nearby Off-Track Betting parlor to place two-dollar Trifecta bets. We never won, but it was one of the special things we did as friends.

In addition to my friends at SUNY Farmingdale, I had gained a steady girlfriend named Patti. I had seen her around the campus, and she frequently visited one of her friends in my dormitory building. My friends thought she was beautiful and spoke of her every time they saw her in the dorm. She had jet-black hair, brown eyes, and a friendly smile for me whenever we passed one another. I never thought about her beyond that because I never thought she would ever want to go out with me anyway.

We formally met at a Halloween party held in my dormitory. Mickey had taken a train in from Jackson Heights to attend. I dressed as a hobo. I wore an old winter hat and torn clothes and scuffed some charcoal on my face. The disguise enabled me to talk to Patti more easily. We met again a few weeks later at the campus bar and spoke to one another for hours. From that point on, we were inseparable. She loved me despite my quirks and sensitivity. The love we shared helped me grow and heal in many ways.

I once brought Patti into Jackson Heights to meet my father in one of the Irish bars. He was delighted to see her and immediately started talking in an Irish brogue and singing little bits of Irish songs. He seemed to be putting on a show for her—and insisted on ordering her a stinger, a cocktail made from crème de menthe and brandy. She wasn't used to drinking the strong stuff, but politely did her best to finish the drink. I could tell she was affected by the alcohol, and I cautiously wondered why my father was intent on getting Patti drunk. He then ordered another stinger for her, and she did her best to finish that one, too. She was now so drunk that she struggled to walk and talk. My father then ordered an Irish coffee for her, to "wake her up." I realized I had to get her out of the bar, and we were fortunate enough to catch a late-night train back to college.

****

My father came out to watch me get my associate's degree. When he saw me, he beamed with pride. The moment was wonderful for me as well. After many years of watching his Jekyll and Hyde behavior, I was unsure of what to expect. If he got drunk, he became bitter and belligerent. If he remained sober, he was charming and fun. To celebrate, he took Patti and me out to dinner at a diner across the street from the college. He dressed in a suit and didn't get drunk or try to get us drunk. He even gave me $200 as a graduation gift.

As he got into a cab to go back to the train station, he said goodbye to us in his Irish brogue and made sure to add, "Now don't fuck this up, son!"

87

I wanted to stay in college, so I added all my zeros to the financial aid forms again and enrolled at the State University of New York at Cortland, where I would major in biology. The college was near Patti's home in Syracuse, and she joined me at Cortland the following semester.

College was a home for me, and I couldn't afford to screw up. Being there kept me insulated from real-world craziness. I visited the Healys in Delaware every Christmas and Thanksgiving. Knowing they were always there for me was enough to keep me hopeful about my future. I had a bicycle for local travel, and whenever I needed to, I hitchhiked to Long Island, Upstate New York, Pennsylvania, and Delaware. I scratched away at every source of financial aid I could find, and I took out student loans to get me through the summers. One summer, my student loan had not been processed on time, and I had to miss some meals for several days. I became so hungry that I walked to a nearby Pizza Hut to beg for food. A young waitress greeted me at the front of the restaurant.

I asked, "Do you have any extra food, like if someone only ate half of their pizza and left the rest, that I could eat?"

The waitress brought over the manager, and I told him I was simply broke and starving. He walked up close to me and spoke in a low voice, murmuring, "You can have anything you want. Stay here for a moment, and I'll get a table set up for you."

I was so touched. I started crying right in front of him.

He seated me, and a waitress soon arrived with a freshly made pizza pie and an ice-cold pitcher of Coca-Cola, just for me. While I was eating, the manager came over to remind me, "Don't forget, you have full access to the salad bar, too."

88

Through occasional phone calls and letters, I could piece together a general sense of where my siblings were. I learned that Dennis had to have open heart surgery to repair a congenital heart defect called a "patent ductus arteriosus." He later enlisted in the Army and was stationed near the DMZ in Korea. He was sending money back to the States to support Katie, who was trying to earn an associate degree in chemical technology.

Pat and Mickey were living at my father's apartment in Jackson Heights. They struggled to find work and occasionally did odd jobs or, in Mickey's case, coerced unsuspecting citizens to donate their money. Mickey even robbed guys who ran "Three Card Monte" games in Manhattan.

Pat and Mickey visited me once while I was in college at Cortland. Billy McNally drove them up from New York City in a snowstorm. They arrived with several cases of beer, which we drank while playing darts and hanging out in my dorm room with a few other friends. The inability to predict how Mickey might behave, especially if he was drunk or high, was a common source of anxiety for me. He tended to get emotionally distraught when drunk—and I was afraid he'd meltdown, get into a wild fight, or say something crazy to one of my friends. I loved Mickey and hated myself for feeling that way, but I did.

THE RIVER

As the night went on, many other parties started on my floor, and after a while, I lost track of where my brothers were. The parties lasted well past midnight. Dozens of drunk students roamed the halls and drifted from one room to the next. Eventually, a student sprinted into my room with a panicked look on his face.

"Yo dude, your brothers are shit-faced! They're beating the crap out of each other in my room right now!" he announced.

I ran to his room and saw my brothers were indeed fighting each other. The altercation had spilled into the hallway and included punches to the face, strangleholds, kicks, and ripped clothes. Dozens of people stood around and watched the fight, strictly for entertainment. I was able to break my brothers apart just as campus police arrived.

The next day, one of the students who lived in my dorm came into my room to speak with me. He seemed to feel awkward about doing so but clearly had something on his mind.

"Hey, Kev. I gotta tell you something, man."

"What's up?" I asked.

"I don't know, man. It's about your brother."

"Yeah, what? What about him?"

"Nothing, it's nothing really, but— "

"Come on, man," I interrupted. "Just spit it out."

"I don't want to get too personal or anything, but I wanted to tell you that when I woke up after the party, I saw your brother Pat drinking beer from all the cups that were left around. It was a lot of beer, dude ... a *lot*."

I knew Pat was an alcoholic, but I still acted surprised when I heard this. A few weeks later, I went to the campus psychologist and told him how distraught I was about Pat and his struggle with alcoholism. I asked the psychologist to recommend a place where my brother could get treatment. The psychologist suggested a facility affiliated with the Upstate Medical Center in Syracuse. He said that, given Pat's financial situation, the clinic might admit Pat for free. I called Pat and told him about the place and the opportunity. He agreed to try the program out, and took a bus from New York to Cortland, where we met to talk for a while before he took another bus up to Syracuse. Prior to boarding the bus for the forty-five-minute ride to Syracuse, Pat bought a six-pack of sixteen-ounce beers. About a week later, I called the clinic in Syracuse. A young woman answered the phone.

"Hi, I'm Kevin Weadock," I said. "Pat Weadock is my brother. I was wondering if I could speak with him."

"I'm sorry, but your brother is no longer here," she said.

"But he just got there," I insisted. "Are you sure?"

"I'm sorry, Mr. Weadock, but your brother left the day after he enrolled in the program. He jumped out of his bedroom window. We haven't seen him since, so he is no longer eligible to participate in the program."

89

I had many friends at SUNY Cortland, most of whom were foreign students majoring in one form of engineering or another. Those friendships eventually led me to think I might be able to study engineering as well. Although I was too far along in my biology major to switch, I was serious about becoming an engineer, so I took calculus III, differential equations, and a few other courses that were required for all engineering students. In my final semester at Cortland, I applied to the graduate biomedical engineering programs at Rensselaer Polytechnic Institute and Rutgers University. By May, I hadn't heard from either of them, and I was resigned to start looking for a job as a biologist—or anything, really. I took great pride in the fact that I had earned a bachelor's degree in biology, and spent a few weeks looking for a job near Patti's house in Syracuse. Without a car, I didn't have a chance.

While Patti stayed in Syracuse, I visited my father in Jackson Heights. Pat and Mickey were working as carpenters in Manhattan, so I hoped my father might be able to help me land a job, too. In just a few days, he brought me up to one of the top floors of a skyscraper he was working on in midtown Manhattan and introduced me to a bunch of men from the Local 608 Carpenters Union. They were in what my father called a shanty, a makeshift locker room where they put on their boots and dusty clothes and threw down a few shots of whiskey to start the day.

"Hey, Johnny!" my father yelled. "I'd like to introduce you to my college boy."

"Oh, he's a helluva lad, Paddy."

Johnny was a huge man, and when he shook my hand, I realized there were two types of men in this world: men who worked for a living—and guys like me.

"So, what would you be studying at college, son?" Johnny asked.

"Biology," I answered.

"That's the thing with the guts, Johnny," my father explained.

"Oh, so you're gonna be a doctor, are ya?" Johnny challenged.

"Well, maybe," I replied. "I hope."

Within hours, I was in another skyscraper, the Citicorp Building on East 53rd Street and Lexington Avenue. My job was to load sheetrock off a truck and onto an elevator that ran up the outside of the building. The elevator was just a moving platform, and I could have easily fallen off. On my first trip up to the fiftieth floor, a seven-foot-tall guy named "Tiny" warned me to watch my head and arms so they didn't get clipped off on the way up. He also warned me not to kick any loose sheetrock, wood, or other materials off the platform because falling debris could kill people on the street below. By the time I got off the elevator on the fiftieth floor, I felt like quitting.

"Are you OK, man?" Tiny asked.

"I'm afraid of heights," I mumbled. "I didn't know this job involved crazy heights like this."

He stated, "Well, either you can do it—or you can't. We'll try one more trip up and down and see how you feel.

THE RIVER

If you're not up to it, you'll have to leave the site. There are plenty of guys waiting to get your job."

I mustered up the courage to stay on the elevator and gradually learned to love the job. I began to think that being a construction worker might not be so bad after all. During this time, I got to see my father in ways I never had before. I saw that the sober version of my father was nothing like the drunk version. When sober, he read books by James Joyce. He read at least one newspaper each morning and did his best to complete *The New York Times* crossword puzzle on Sunday. He had a knack for geometry, and the Local 608 Carpenters Union considered him a master carpenter. He liked to joke around with people on the job site. Just having time with my father during the fraction of the day when he was sober seemed to increase my self-confidence. I started thinking that guys who had sober fathers may have had an edge on me.

I caught myself daydreaming one afternoon during a lunch break. I was sitting on a bench outside a delicatessen in Manhattan and eating my typical lunch: a roast beef sandwich and a quart of orange juice. I wondered what my life would have been like if my parents weren't alcoholics. I imagined my whole family sitting on lawn chairs at a barbecue in the backyard of a nice home in Rockaway Beach, all of us healthy and happy. Maybe this version of my family existed in a parallel universe. Maybe I'd meet them all, after I died. Maybe they would fold us into their family. Or maybe they would look down on us.

90

As he did his entire adult life, my father went straight from work to one of many Irish bars in Manhattan for a few shots of whiskey with his coworkers. When he got off the train in Jackson Heights, he went straight to one of many Irish bars within steps of the subway station. He bounced from one bar to another until ten or eleven at night. On his way back to the apartment, he grabbed a slice of pizza and a chocolate candy bar—his usual dinner. He kept very little food in his refrigerator except an occasional chunk of sharp cheddar cheese and a jar of spicy mustard.

On one of the nights I was alone in the apartment, I was alerted to my father's arrival by the sounds of his incoherent voice and stumbling as he walked up the stairs. By the time he burst through the front door, he was ranting loudly, almost yelling. He planted his feet in front of me so his face was just inches from mine. I looked at the anger in his eyes and how square and chiseled his face was. I could see clearly my father was indeed a rough person, far from the soft-spoken professors and jovial friends I had come to know in college.

"What's wrong, Dad?" I questioned.

"I'll tell you what's wrong," he bellowed. "You've got aunts and uncles that could be your hook. They could bring you up into one of their organizations. You've got dozens of cousins, all around you, all very successful, the likes of which you can't even fucking imagine!"

I had heard it all before. I planned to just let him run through the usual diatribe; I hoped we could have something resembling a normal conversation afterward—but then I changed my mind and asked, "I've never really seen them, Dad. How come we've never met them?"

"Oh, you sure have. Your Aunt Sis in Rockaway and your Uncle Walter in Riverdale."

"That's it, Dad?" I prodded. "I met them when I was a kid. They weren't responsible for us, anyway."

"Oh, now don't be putting this shit on me, son. They're all out there, right here in this big fucking city. And you don't even know *one* of them!"

"No, I don't."

"They're all up in Rockaway, Manhattan, and the Bronx, and you can't believe how much they could help you, but you've gone ahead and fucked yourselves up!"

"*I'm* not fucked up, Dad," I insisted.

"Everything in our lives is fucked up, son," he growled. "Your mother has destroyed us all. The filthy whore! And your brothers and your sister too—up there in Saskatchewan or whatever the fuck that little town of hillbillies is . . ."

"Katie lives in Catskill," I provided.

"Who gives a flying fuck where they are? They've gone ahead and destroyed themselves, too. They're no good to nobody now—no way, no how."

As I started to walk away from him, he adjusted his stance so he could continue yelling into my face. He laughed, "You know, you're not gonna live forever, son!"

"I know, Dad."

"One day, someone is going to put a bullet *right here*." He finished the statement by pushing a stiff finger into the center of my forehead.

The force of his finger shoved my head into the wall behind me. He then went into a crouch and threw a wild punch at my face. I moved my head just enough to avoid the blow, which was thrown with a force that might have broken my jaw or knocked me out. His fist hit the wall behind me, causing him to pull his hand back to his chest and lean over, groaning. He then went into his bedroom and lay down. He had done similar things with my brothers when he was drunk, including kicking and punching them when they weren't looking. He had even pointed a loaded Walther PP .32 pistol at Mickey's head.

Angry and confused, I left—without waiting around to say goodbye to Pat or Mickey or letting the foreman on my job know I quit. I walked down to the Woodside train station to board a late-night train out to Billy McNally's house. I was welcome at Billy's house; his family treated me like one of their own. I spent many nights that summer crashing at Billy's, usually in his handicapped van, which had a bed. His family kidded me about it and started referring to the van as "Kevin's Condo."

91

In late August, Mickey called me from a phone booth in one of the Irish bars in Jackson Heights to tell me I had received an acceptance letter from the biomedical engineering program at Rutgers University. I'd been staying at the McNallys', and Billy offered to drive me to the Rutgers campus in New Brunswick, New Jersey. I showed up with a large black trunk full of books, clothes, and miscellaneous personal stuff.

A few weeks after I arrived, Donna surprised me by driving my mother's car out from Pennsylvania to visit. It was the only time she ever visited me in any of the places I lived. She showed up outside my dormitory with a big smile on her face.

"Hey, Kevin."

"Wow, Donna, you're all grown up!"

"Well, that's what happens, Kevin. We're *all* getting older!" she kidded.

She was nineteen years old, and her hair was still as blonde as ever. The moment was bittersweet for me. I didn't know how to deal with my feelings about not being able to grow up with her. I loved her ... but I hardly knew her. We had lunch in a diner near the Rutgers campus, and she told me that, without a High School diploma, she hadn't had any luck finding a job in Pennsylvania. I learned she had a serious relationship going on with a guy, too.

While we talked, Donna stared at me for a few seconds, then fidgeted with things on the table, and then went back to staring at me. I didn't know whether she was just shy or if something was bothering her.

"What's going on, Donna?"

"It's hard to explain," she admitted. "But I wanted to talk to you about it because it's been bothering me a lot. Mom said you know about the body and medical stuff."

"It's OK, Donna—you can tell me," I assured her.

"Sometimes, I think I'm going crazy," she laughed.

"Why do you say that?" I asked.

"I don't know why, but sometimes I hear voices in my head. It scares the hell out of me."

"Is it *your* voice that you hear?" I wondered.

"No. It's just ... different people," she muttered, looking down at the table.

"It's probably stress, Donna," I comforted. "Sometimes, stress can be so bad that people get depressed or start having other problems, like anxiety and stuff."

"You think so?" she prodded, her tone hopeful.

"Yes, definitely. You know, sometimes, I feel like I'm going crazy, too. It's probably just stress."

92

I was able to secure some financial aid and an academic scholarship to cover tuition and housing, but I had to work in a pool hall to earn money for food and other living expenses. I lived in graduate housing with three other students. Two of them were from China, and the other was from India. I wasn't making enough money to feed myself adequately, and I eventually resorted to stealing onions and rice from them while they slept. I still lost ten pounds during my first semester. At six feet, one inch in height, I weighed 155 pounds.

During my second semester at Rutgers, a fellow biomedical engineering student named Michael Dunn saw me working in the pool hall.

"Why are you working *here*?" he asked. "Don't you have a research fellowship or something?"

I replied, "No, why?"

"How will you be able to write a thesis without doing research?" he wondered.

"Oh shit!" I exclaimed. "I didn't know I needed one."

Mike laughed and then told me he knew of an open research fellowship position in the Pathology Department of Rutgers Medical School, which was where he worked. He introduced me to his advisor, a professor who looked like he was just a few years older than me. His lab was developing an artificial skin for treating third-degree burns. The professor showed me a few medical journals that had color photographs of children who suffered third-degree burns over large portions of their body. The photographs haunted me—I couldn't fathom the pain the children and their families must have experienced. It was all I needed to commit myself to the work in the lab.

Unlike me, Mike had been an excellent student in high school and had earned a full academic scholarship to Boston University to study biomedical engineering. I learned Mike was one of nine children and that he grew up in a small Cape Cod home in Milford, Connecticut. His father worked nights in a factory, and his mother stayed home to raise him and his siblings.

Mike and I decided to share an apartment in New Brunswick. Since neither of us had a car, we used our bicycles to carry most of our stuff to our new place. For furniture, I walked around the streets of New Brunswick in search of items people were throwing out. I found a queen-size foam mattress a few blocks away and dragged it back to the apartment. Mike decided to keep using the fold-up cot he'd slept on in his prior "apartment," a landing he rented in a stairwell.

With the money I earned from the research fellowship, I started to eat better again—with the singular goal of gaining weight. I ate calzones, French toast, milk shakes, Heinekens, pizza, ice cream, and anything else that might help me gain weight.

93

About thirty minutes into my visit, I realized my mother didn't have a can of beer in front of her. I waited for her to get up and get one from the refrigerator, but it never happened. I didn't know what triggered the change, but my mother had stopped drinking. Our conversation was different this time. She seemed to want to tell me about her life, as though she thought the information was important for me to know.

She told me her great-grandmother was a Native American who lived on an Ojibwe reservation in Wisconsin. This was exciting for me to hear! All I had ever heard about my ancestry was I was Irish and Irish and Irish. Although my mother had moved on to other topics, I kept thinking there might be a thin thread of Native American genes in my body. I thought about Mickey, who had dark eyes and high cheekbones and very little facial hair. I thought about how he'd had no fear hanging out of the seventy-seventh floor of the World Trade Tower. I had green eyes and brown hair, but I hoped I had little bits of Ojibwe in me somewhere as well.

I learned more about my mother's childhood and her time in a reform school.

"Wow. You lived in a reform school?"

"Yes, I did," she laughed. "I think my mother just needed a break from me. I was a wild child, Kevin!"

"How long were you there?"

"A little over a year, I think."

"And where was your father?"

"He drank a lot. My mother threw him out, and he wound up working on oil pipelines somewhere in Alaska. Whatever money he made he spent on booze. We got nothing at all from him."

"I didn't know that about him. I thought he was nice."

"Well, he *was* nice, when he wasn't drunk," she chuckled. "He showed up one day at our house again, begging to be let in."

"Were you still in reform school?" I asked.

"Yes, but he came and got me."

"You sound like you didn't want to go back home."

"I loved my sisters Linda and Donna ... and your Uncle Mike—but when I was young, I didn't get along with my father at all. I was so mad at him for what he did to us—I couldn't stand to be in the same house with him. I ran away to New York just a couple of days after I got home. I was sixteen, almost seventeen."

"Oh, so that's how you guys met?" I asked, figuring my father was about to make his first appearance in her life story.

"Yep. That's where we met. But I almost didn't meet him, Kev."

"What do you mean?"

She stopped talking for a while. I remained quiet, hoping she would pick up the conversation again. When she did, she drawled, "I was living in a room with another girl in Chelsea, above a bar on the corner of 10th Avenue and 19th Street. I was very lost and depressed. I spent an afternoon sitting at the end of a pier on the Hudson River, deciding whether I should just jump in—just end it all, you know?"

"I'm glad you didn't, Mom."

She admitted, "To be honest, I'm not sure what made me stand up and walk back into the city—but I did."

She said she soon met my thirty-two-year-old father, literally bumping into him as they walked up 10th Avenue in Chelsea.

"Oh, he was a handsome man, Kevin," she recalled as she shook her head from side to side.

"Swept me right off my feet. We moved in together almost immediately. I was so in love with him."

"When did he tell you about his family in Ireland?" I asked.

"Years later, Kev—just after you were born. It changed our whole relationship. I never really trusted him after that."

94

My mother's place sat alongside four other bungalows on a dirt road that came off a county road at the base of the Appalachian Trail. It served as a home for all my siblings—regardless of emotional state, sobriety, or employment status. Sobriety enabled my mother to purchase a second bungalow next to hers, and my siblings lived in that bungalow from time to time as well.

Her sobriety also illuminated the fact that my mother was a badass. She was direct with neighbors, family, and everyone else. Mickey married, and despite her struggle to maintain her mental health, so had Donna. They had two children each, and my mother helped raise all four of them. She pushed back on the cycle of enablement and its insidious sequelae. She sought financial support from any adult living in either of her bungalows. I believe her sobriety may have motivated Pat to stop drinking as well.

****

I stopped in to see her on a sweltering hot summer day. She sat on an old couch in the second bungalow, exhausted. She leaned over to take off her dirty white sneakers, which had holes in the toes, and then leaned her head back against the wall. A large stand-up fan stationed several feet away blew air on her face. A half dozen little kids ran in and out of the bungalow.

"This is just like Rockaway Beach," she laughed.

"Why?" I asked. "What do you mean?"

Still laughing, she explained, "I had all you kids running around ... the diapers, the laundry—just one thing to another, in a blur. It never stopped."

"I couldn't do it. I can barely take care of myself!" I admitted.

"I slept a few hours here and there, but I always had to be on guard," my mother declared. "Deep down, I knew I couldn't keep up. You kids were always running around—I just crossed my fingers and hoped for the best. I was afraid one of you might get killed or lost. I loved you all so very much. Drinking helped me sleep and deal with the craziness. But it all got mixed in together ... drinking, sleeping, taking care of you kids, dealing with your father—I was completely overwhelmed sometimes. After a moment of reflection, she laughed and said, "What am I talking about? I was overwhelmed *all* the time!"

"I can only imagine, Mom."

"Even drinking didn't help. I couldn't drink enough to stay sane. Did you know I was hospitalized a few times, Kevy?"

"Yeah, I remember something like that," I answered.

After a minute or so of silence, my mother started talking again, insisting, "Your father and I *did* love each other—you know?"

"Not really, but I guess you must have, to have had all of us kids," I agreed.

"You've heard the expression about how there's a thin line between love and hate?" she asked.

"Yep," I confirmed.

She stated, "Well, that was us."

While she reminisced, I noticed her feet were calloused and caked with dirt.

"Hey, Mom," I interrupted. "You look like you could use a foot massage."

"Oh, please don't look at my feet."

"Seriously, Mom. I could give you one right now."

"Really?"

"Sure, why not?"

In a tired voice, she agreed, "That would be wonderful, Kevin."

I had no idea how to give a foot massage, but my mother was going to get one, no matter what. I found a large metal pot that looked like it had been in use during the Civil War, and I filled it with warm water and some shampoo. She placed her feet in the pot of soapy water and tilted her head back against the wall again. I rubbed the dirt off her feet and then massaged them as we talked about the latest drama in everyone's lives. The little kids ran in and out of the house, yelling and tripping and crying and occasionally stopping to speak to my mother.

"Forget about the kids for a while, Mom. Just try to relax, alright?"

"I'm doing my best, Kev."

"Is this foot massage helping?"

"Oh, you have no idea, Kevin. Thank you, thank you, thank you."

"No problem, Mom."

95

Patti and I got married a month after I earned my master's degree in biomedical engineering. Her father paid for a huge wedding at the Tuscarora country club in Syracuse. It was a beautiful fall day, and my biological and foster families met Patti's huge extended family for the first time. It was also the day my biological family got to see Anne again, the first time since she was an infant. Billy McNally was my best man.

The photographer spent hours taking pictures of Patti and me and our families, separately and together, with dozens of photos of my biological family and the Healys together as well. I imagined it was an awkward but wonderful moment for all of them, especially Anne Healy, who was fifteen at the time. I spent the entire day preoccupied with thoughts of Anne, Margaret Healy, and my mother. I worried Anne's outward expressions of joy masked confusion and pain. The Healys watched Anne physically cling to her biological family, and my mother spent most of the day looking at Anne. My father didn't show up. The two-hundred-mile trip and prospect of having to face everyone else in one sitting were enough to keep him in Jackson Heights.

Patti and I left Syracuse the next day and we spent our honeymoon in Acapulco. I was back at Rutgers the following week. I asked my advisor if I could try to earn a

PhD degree. He said he wasn't sure if my engineering background was strong enough to get through the program, but he would be willing to take a chance on me if I *immediately* began studying for the PhD qualifying exam. He said I needed a "head-start" on the exam, which was a year away. If I passed, he would support me in his lab until I graduated. Patti and I rented an apartment on the Rutgers campus, and she quickly found a job just a few miles away.

The qualifying exam consisted of four sections: mammalian physiology, general engineering, biomedical engineering, and biomaterials. Questions from the general engineering section could come from any course related to engineering: mechanics, physics, circuit theory, computer design, digital signal processing, and any branch of mathematics. Mike and I studied together for several hours each day, almost every day, for the next year. I studied a similar amount of time by myself at night.

Each part of the exam was three hours long; the first six hours were held on a Friday, and the next six hours were held the following Monday. Six PhD candidates took the exam that year—only Mike and I passed. We were the first students in three years to do so. After all the results were posted, I learned I received a grade of 66 in the general engineering section of the test—one point above the required grade of 65.

It took three more years to complete the research required to write and defend my doctoral dissertation. I developed a model for how large molecules move through collagen membranes. The work could be used to test the feasibility of using collagen as a drug-delivery matrix. I didn't know whether my research would stand up to the scrutiny of the professors on my committee. Some, or all, of my experiments might need to be repeated—sending me on a long, confounding journey to nowhere. I was also required to publish various aspects of my work in at least three different peer-reviewed journals. I was constantly worried I wouldn't make it.

****

Along with Kris, Timmy, and Dennis, my mother came to my graduation event at the Rutgers Athletic Center. The facility was huge, with enough seating for 8,000 people. Margaret and Tom Healy were also there with Eileen and Anne. Patti and her parents, plus a few sisters *and* her niece were there as well. They all sat together in the upper deck. Hundreds of other graduate students and I sat on folding chairs placed on the floor of the facility. Students waited for their name to be called before walking up to the stage to receive their degree and shake hands with the President of Rutgers University.

It took forever to get to the students with last names beginning with W. As the announcer started calling out the names that began with W, my heart began pounding. I reflected on the fact that I had been in college for ten years! As I walked to the stage, I heard my family cheer me on.

I even heard my mother yell, "Yay, Kevy!"

96

My singular focus had been to stay in college for as long as I could. If there was another degree beyond a PhD, I would have tried to get that too. I rarely thought about what my life would be like after I graduated. Because Patti already had a promising job nearby, I chose to stay in the familiar environment of Rutgers University and work as a part-time technician in a few labs there. Although I was twenty-seven years old, I still didn't have a driver's license or a car. I bought a rusty old Dodge Omni for $500 and spray-painted the rust with green paint—just a shade or two away from the car's actual color.

I also decided I'd try to help my brothers form a construction company. I called it Weadock Brothers, Inc. I had business cards made and circulars printed up, and I placed them in the mailbox of any house that looked like it needed work. I convinced one of the professors on my doctoral committee to advance me $3,000 for painting his house and replacing its roof. I promptly bought a beat-up pickup truck and a bunch of tools. I gave both to my brothers, and they did an excellent job painting the professor's house and replacing his roof. We were able to get more jobs in the professor's neighborhood, and we even replaced the roof on my friend Mike's house too. This eventually led to jobs in surrounding towns and others back in Pennsylvania as well.

My brothers loved to work. I sensed their pride as they bounced around the job site with a pencil on their ear and belts full of tools. I watched in awe as they carried 70-pound bundles of shingles on their backs, up a ladder, and onto the roof. I watched them hammer nails through the shingles for hours and hours under the hot sun. I thought *I* was in great physical condition, but immediately realized I couldn't do *this* work. While their hands were rough and marked with cuts and calluses, mine were relatively clean and soft. It pained me to see that each of my brothers were missing a few teeth, and many of their remaining teeth were chipped or discolored. The state of their teeth was a painful reminder of the divergence in our lives. The Healy's were good about getting me to the dentist regularly, and many of my teeth were now stuffed with fillings. I was even able to get crowns on my molars, courtesy of Patti's dental insurance.

It saddened me to know my brothers had adapted to working like this. For as hard as they worked, they were still poor. I wanted to help them in any way I could. I fetched lunch and drinks, helped them move things on the ground, and handed them tools. I took nothing from the money we earned. I kept looking for new customers.

When Mickey began to miss days on the job, I knew something was wrong. I assumed it was drugs, but I never really knew what drugs he was taking. He reluctantly admitted to me that he had developed an addiction to cocaine. He had stolen two ounces of cocaine from a drug dealer in Jackson Heights earlier that year—and snorted it all by himself.

Pat's sobriety let our relationship bloom into what we had both hoped it could be. We weren't afraid to hug or say we loved each other. He quickly emerged as the true leader of our little venture. Pat seemed to be able to do anything. He not only played multiple instruments, wrote music, rebuilt car engines, and fixed appliances, but also knew how to build patios, walkways, and housing additions. I felt like an idiot compared to him.

On one of the days I was helping my brothers, I started talking with a mason who was working on the same house. Our conversation drifted from one topic to another and eventually wound up on the subject of his lower-back pain. I offered up a brief description of spinal anatomy and explained that a bulging disc might be causing his sciatica.

"Hey, you seem pretty smart," he remarked. "Did you go to college or something?"

I decided right then and there that I needed to be much more aggressive in looking for a job. The fate of Weadock Brothers, Inc., was now in Pat's hands. I set a goal of sending out one hundred résumés. Since Patti enjoyed her current job, I only sent them to nearby universities and companies. It didn't matter. I was invited to only a few interviews, and just an hour or so into each, I knew I didn't have a chance. They wanted experience. Or they wanted a biologist. Or an engineer. But not both. Or something else. Whatever they wanted—I wasn't it.

****

Over a year had passed since I graduated. One summer night, I found myself sitting in my car outside a building on the edge of the Rutgers campus. I was listening to a Yankees game on the radio. When the game ended, I heard crickets' chirping in the little patches of woods nearby, and my thoughts started to turn against me, spiraling into self-doubt—and then anger. I feared I wasted all those years in college. I yelled at my reflection in the rearview mirror. I punched the side of my head a few times, making sure to hurt myself by using my knuckles as the leading edge of my fist against my temple. Eventually, I just fell asleep in my car.

A few months later, Margaret and Tom Healy unexpectedly visited Patti and me at our apartment. They were coming back from visiting their relatives in New York, and thought it would be fun to surprise us. I was shocked to see them, and as soon as I opened the door, Margaret Healy burst in with hugs and kisses. We sat around our small kitchen table and drank tea as we caught up.

"Any leads on a job yet, Kevin?" Tom Healy asked.

"Not yet, Dad, but I'm still looking," I replied.

"My Lord!" Margaret Healy exclaimed. "You'd think the whole world would be looking for someone like you, Love."

I joked, "Well, they haven't found me yet, Mom."

"They will, Love. Isn't that right, Tommy?"

"Definitely, Maise," Tom Healy agreed, looking at me as he spoke.

97

Dr. Kassis was sitting down when I walked into his office, which was surprisingly small. He was a middle-aged man with a small amount of black hair on the sides of his otherwise bald head, and he wore glasses and a mustache. He stood up and came over to shake my hand, introducing himself as Amin. We talked about so many things that I forgot I was in an interview. I told him about a paperback book my brother Pat and I had passed back and forth to each other over the years, a cartoon-like book about Einstein's theory of relativity. Amin spoke to me about his work with Auger electrons and the isotope Iodine[125]. He also talked about some experiences he had during graduate school at McGill University in Montreal. I told him about a couple of patents on which I was an inventor.

"I saw that," he said, tapping his finger on my résumé.

He told me about his interest in patenting his ideas and his frustration in trying to find a business partner for one of his first inventions—a vacuum cleaner for a swimming pool.

"Getting a patent is one thing," he claimed. "Almost anyone can invent *something*. It's what you do with it that matters."

I tried to be as open and honest as I possibly could, telling him I was currently doing odd jobs in a couple of labs at Rutgers and I'd even started a roofing and siding company with my brothers. I really didn't think I had a shot at getting the position, so I just relaxed and enjoyed our conversation. I hoped he might give me some advice on what I could do to find a job.

Amin said the person he was looking to hire would have to design a system for the radiopharmacy in the Brigham and Women's Hospital—a system that could attach large amounts of radioactive iodine to monoclonal antibodies. Whoever got the job would personally have to use the system and be present when the doses were administered to patients suffering from advanced ovarian cancer. I told him I had dreamed of studying new ways to treat cancer and that I had even worked with radiation before, albeit in much smaller amounts.

At the end of the interview, Amin said that he enjoyed speaking with me. He said he was impressed that I had already published five papers and was an inventor on two patents. He then showed me a one-inch stack of résumés he had received from people who were applying for the fellowship. He positioned the stack on the desk in front of him, holding it with two hands. He said he wouldn't look at another résumé—*if* I would accept the position right there and then.

"Well, yes," I agreed. "I *definitely* want this position. Thank you."

Standing up and reaching over his desk to shake my hand, he declared, "Welcome to Harvard Medical School."

I was hired as a postdoctoral research fellow, with just an outside chance of becoming a professor there. The opportunity to be part of a team that was trying to develop a new way to treat cancer was a dream come true. Patti and

I agreed that she would continue working in New Jersey while I lived in Boston.

Amin wasted no time getting me started in the lab. He demonstrated how they were currently labeling the monoclonal antibodies, and he explained that the amount of radiation was too much for anyone to handle on a regular basis without the risk of being exposed to harmful levels. I began working with several other research fellows, all of whom were physicians completing fellowships in gynecologic oncology. I eventually developed a remote radiolabeling system that allowed us to treat patients with larger amounts of radiation linked to monoclonal antibodies. The radiolabeled monoclonal antibodies bound specifically to ovarian cancer cells, thereby exposing them to radiation and killing them. This approach was promising because non-cancer tissue received a much lower dose of radiation.

The patients traveled from all over the country to enroll in our clinical trial. All of them had already been through one or more major surgical procedures and several rounds of chemotherapy—only to have their cancer return. The first patient who I was involved with treating was a thirty-two-year-old woman named Donna. She had driven up from Georgia with her husband. Since her husband was a fireman, a fire department in Boston agreed to house him while Donna was hospitalized.

During the preparation of the sample used to treat her, our Geiger counter, which we referred to as "the squawk box," screamed out its trademark warnings. To protect myself, I placed all the reactants and vessels behind lead bricks I previously placed inside a vented glove box. The only way I could see whether the reactants were moving correctly through the reaction vessels was by looking into a mirror placed behind the vessels. The only time my hands were exposed to the radiation was when I had to push long needles into the reaction vessels. Despite all the time we spent developing our system to reduce my exposure to radiation, my hands *still* shook.

"Breathe, Kevin," coached a gynecologic oncology fellow as I tried to complete the process. His voice was calm and confident.

"I just can't stop my hands from shaking," I remarked.

"But we've already worked this out, Kevin," he laughed. "It's safe—even if your hands *are* shaking," he kidded.

The sound of his voice and laughter calmed me down.

After the reaction was complete, I removed a small amount of the sample for testing. Before injecting it into a patient, we needed to know whether the sample was sterile and whether the radioactive isotope I^{131} was linked to the monoclonal antibody. If the I^{131} was still "free," it couldn't target the tumor. Once we confirmed the product was sterile, and radiolabelling did indeed occur, I put the product in a lead container the size of a sixteen-ounce beer can. We put it on a cart and wheeled it up to the room where Donna and her husband waited. Hospital security guards cleared the way for us, ensuring other people weren't unnecessarily exposed. When Donna saw us enter the room with the cart, she stopped talking, took a deep breath, and hugged her husband.

I was asked to leave the room while a doctor delivered the radiolabeled monoclonal antibody through a port in Donna's abdominal wall. I walked outside her room and went into a bathroom that was only about fifteen feet away. I locked the door and was immediately overcome with emotion. I desperately wanted Donna to live.

THE RIVER

98

While I lived in Boston, Pat completed his associate's degree in electronic technology and moved in with Katie in Beacon, New York. He had graduated with a 3.96 grade point average—second in his class. Katie had earned an associate's degree in chemical technology the year before. Both were now employed by IBM in East Fishkill, New York. Now sober for a few years, Pat developed a passion for long-distance running. He loved his job at IBM and developed a hobby of building simple robots at home. Having a job and a car enabled Pat to visit me in Boston a few times. We toured the city's well-known landmarks including the New England Aquarium, the Museum of Fine Arts, and Faneuil Hall.

Pat was most interested in visiting the USS Constitution Museum, and we ate at the Union Oyster House afterwards. We sat at a small C-shaped wooden bar that was hundreds of years old. As we waited to be served some clams, we leaned forward on the bar—our forearms exposed. I couldn't help but notice the dozens of scars on Pat's arms—scars from self-inflicted cuts and attempts to kill himself when he was a teenager. I had seen them before but always looked away—I just couldn't think about them. But I was ready to look at them now. I wondered just how much pain Pat had experienced. I teared up thinking about how amazing Pat was—about his strength and courage to get to this wonderful moment in our lives.

During one of his visits, Pat told me Dennis and Timmy were still doing roofing and siding jobs in Pennsylvania—but not for Weadock Brothers, Inc., which had folded several months before I moved to Boston. He also said Donna and Mickey were in a psychiatric hospital in Pennsylvania. What little mental health Mickey once possessed had evaporated after he became addicted to cocaine. Donna's doctors were trying to find the right medicine to treat her.

Pat also told me my father had retired and was living off his carpenter's pension—in a second-floor apartment directly above his favorite Irish bar in Jackson Heights. Pat said my father's drinking may have finally caught up with him; that he was acting oddly and was having a hard time remembering things. I called my father just to get a sense of what Pat was talking about. My father took the call from a pay phone located near the back of the bar.

"I'm absolutely fucking delighted you were able to take off out of here like a big-ass bird and make something of yourself, son."

"Thanks, Dad."

"I haven't heard from your sister or any of your brothers in a few years, you know. They've likely gone ahead and destroyed themselves—living with your Momma and the rest of them shit-kicking, stump-jumping, banjo-banging bastards from Pennsylvania."

"They're doing OK too, Dad," I told him. "Pat is living with Katie now upstate. He said he just spoke with you a month or two ago."

"Oh, he did, did he? And what about the Little Giant? Where is he?"

I informed him, "Mickey is in a psychiatric hospital now—somewhere in Pennsylvania."

"Jesus fucking Christ ... that poor bastard. He could have been a master carpenter. I had him all set up in the 608!"

"I think he snorted all that cocaine he stole," I said. "It burned a hole in his nasal septum, and he had to have surgery to fix it. The coke put him over the edge, I think."

"And they're still looking for him, you know? Those bastards put a few bullets right through my front door. Who's gonna pay for that? Me? No way, no how."

I insisted, "It's better that Mickey is in the hospital, Dad. The longer the better."

"And the others?" he inquired, layering on his Irish brogue. *"Seems they've forgotten all about their poor old father."*

"They're all doing OK, Dad," I said.

"You know, this is a helluva ship," he remarked.

"What ship, Dad?"

He laughed, *"Oh, c'mon now, son. This ship has been up and down the Irrawaddy River—and to Rangoon as well. Ah, there's nothing like it. Steady as she goes!"*

99

I thought having my mother visit me in Boston would be great, but because she rarely traveled more than ten miles from her home in Pennsylvania, the scenario seemed improbable. I still called her—telling her I now had "a real job" and that I would love to see her. I let her know I would pay for her airfare and she could stay at my apartment. To my surprise, she agreed and arranged to come up that same week.

When she arrived at Logan Airport, I grabbed her small suitcase with one hand and her hand with my other hand, and I whisked her down the escalator. It was a whimsical, happy moment for both of us. During the cab ride back to my apartment, she laughed about a conversation she had with a woman who sat next to her on the plane.

"So, do you live in Boston?" the woman asked my mother.

"No, I'm just visiting my son up here," my mother answered.

"Oh, how nice!" said the woman.

"He's a doctor," my mother bragged.

"Oh, you must be so proud," the woman said.

"Yes. Yes, I am."

She laughed as she imitated the whole conversation, with her replies played in a pompous, aristocratic tone. As we sat in the back seat of the cab, I tried to point out places I knew throughout the city including Beacon Hill, the Charles River, and Prudential Tower. We were soon in my apartment, a studio on Park Drive in the West Fens section. My unit was on the fourth floor and had a bay window that provided a nice view of the Boston Museum of Art and Prudential Tower.

While I was tidying up my apartment, I noticed my mother was gazing through the window and down Park Drive. To me, the look she wore seemed to be one of real sorrow.

"What are you thinking about?" I asked.

"This street, with its buildings and trees ... and all these young people walking around so fast—it reminds me of a part of Brooklyn where your father and I tried to live before you were born."

"Well, *we* can walk fast too, Mom. Do you want to see where I work?"

"Sure, I'd love to," she said.

We threw our coats on and ventured into the cold gray afternoon. We walked along Avenue Louis Pasteur toward Longwood Avenue, where the medical school was. I couldn't help thinking about other important walks I'd taken with my mother.

"Mom, do you remember the night you took us through the rain storm?" I wondered. "The night we got on the train to Minnesota?"

"Oh, that was so long ago, Kevin. I can't believe you remember that. You were so small. Yes, I remember ... I was holding Donna ..."

I continued, "And the time you took us to that place near the boardwalk ... St. John's, right? You were asking the priest if we could live there?"

"Oh, Kevin, please stop!"

We crossed Longwood Avenue and walked directly to the building that housed my lab and office. I could have walked her around the renowned Harvard Medical School campus, but all I really wanted to do was show her that my name was posted underneath Amin's name outside our lab.

I told her, "Every time I see our last name up there, I imagine it's the same feeling a mountain climber might get after placing their country's flag on the top of Mount Everest."

100

He'd been born just a minute or so earlier. I thought Patti was supposed to do something with him, like breast-feed him or something, or that the nurses were going to take him to the room where all the other babies were and start injecting him with vitamins and other important stuff. I really had no idea what to expect next. I was exhausted from a seven-hour drive from Boston, a drive that passed through the tail end of a nor'easter. A nurse interrupted my confusion by taking him off Patti's chest and handing him to me.

Someone had swaddled him in a blanket, and he was kicking his feet, shivering, and crying. I suddenly knew love at first sight was indeed a real phenomenon. I was afraid he might slip out of my arms or that I might drop him. I almost wanted the nurse to take him away from me — the responsibility of holding him seemed overwhelming.

"Congratulations, Dad," the doctor declared as he snapped off his gloves. "You have a very healthy baby boy!"

"Does he have a name yet?" asked one of the nurses who were helping Patti.

"Kevin Patrick," Patti said, tilting her head to look at me as she said it.

The nurse commented, "Oh, that's a wonderful name."

"Oh, isn't he beautiful Kevin?" Patti remarked.

"Yes, yes he is," I agreed. "He definitely has your eyes."

At some point during his wailing and kicking, he stopped moving and startled me by looking directly into my eyes—for a solid two seconds—before starting his gyrations again. I marveled at how a newborn baby could look so seriously into my eyes. I spent the rest of the day thinking that the brief look was his attempt to communicate an urgent message to me: I *must* realize a new life has started—for both of us.

◊◊◊◊◊

… THE RIVER

Afterword

I was having a hard time understanding Dennis. I initially thought it was a bad connection—or he wasn't speaking directly into the phone. When I realized he was telling me Mickey had just been murdered, I yelled and screamed at him. I guess I thought I could scream the news away.

Pat was diagnosed with advanced melanoma two months after Mickey was killed. He died just six months later. To deal with my grief, I wanted to write a book about *them* and how much I loved them. I wanted to tell the story of how my incredible brothers miraculously survived their chaotic journey through trauma, addiction, and mental illness.

I don't know exactly how or when, but the book became a memoir about the earlier part of *my* life. Initial drafts included details of recurrent nightmares that haunted my sleep for many years, ineffable trauma my siblings experienced, and the sorrow I felt, and still feel, about my family's experience. I eventually chose to omit much of this material and instead venture lightly and quickly into some experiences that told the story anyway.

Of course, my experience is not entirely unique. The role of addiction in disrupting families is well chronicled. Nonetheless, I hope my memoir will help adolescents and young adults living in similar situations.

Made in the USA
Columbia, SC
07 October 2023